GORDON RAMSAY AT HIS BEST

with Roz Denny

photographs by Georgia Glynn Smith

Quadrille

This edition first published in 2006 by
Quadrille Publishing Limited
Alhambra House
27-31 Charing Cross Road
London WC2H 0LS

This edition produced exclusively for:
Ashbury Confectionery Limited
Darwin Road
Willowbrook Industrial Estate
Corby
Northamptonshire NN17 5XZ
Producers of the Gordon Ramsay range of chocolates

Cataloguing in Publication Data: a catalogue record for this
book is available from the British Library.

ISBN-13: 978 184400 439 3
ISBN-10: 1 84400 439 2
Printed in China

notes
• All spoon measures are level unless otherwise stated:
1 teaspoon = 5ml spoon; 1 tablespoon = 15ml spoon.
• Egg sizes are specified where they are critical, otherwise you can
use either large or medium eggs. I recommend free-range eggs. If
you are pregnant or in a vulnerable health group, avoid those
recipes that contain raw egg whites or lightly cooked eggs.
• Ovens should always be preheated to the specified temperature.
Individual ovens can deviate by as much as 10°C from the setting,
either way. Get to know your oven and use an oven thermometer to
check its accuracy. My timings are provided as guidelines, with a
description of colour or texture where appropriate.

contents

Foreword

I am as passionate about food now as I was a decade ago when I opened my first restaurant. I rarely relax, as I'm constantly on the move, seeking new tastes and experimenting with flavour combinations. There is still so much more to discover, to taste and to try out. The success of our menus depends on a balance of popular choices and experimenting with new flavours and ideas to push out the boundaries still further. Perfection of skills and techniques reassures our customers, but constant creativity keeps them coming back for more.

When my chefs and I discuss menus late into the night after service, we must be aware of what raw ingredients are at their best for us to exploit to full advantage. Our decisions are based on the quality of ingredients available at that time, and on the appropriateness of dishes for the time of year. There is no point putting a rich aromatic game stew on a summer menu, for example, when customers want a light dish, even if we could buy perfect game 'out of season' from the other side of the world.

Modern air refrigerator transport has meant seasonal boundaries have become blurred, but I won't use out-of-season foods from another hemisphere unless they are as good as our own home-grown produce in season. Some foods defy all odds to be cultivated in another time zone and their scarcity makes me that much more appreciative when they do take centre stage in my kitchen. They say a good chef is as good as the brigade behind him (yes, yes to that), but good suppliers and producers are where it begins, and I am constantly grateful to mine who share my passion and enthusiasm for good food.

This collection of recipes uses foods at their seasonal best, together with ingredients that are available most of the year round. You should find the recipes relatively straightforward to prepare and cook because foods used in the peak of seasonal supply and perfection are best cooked simply. The book begins with personal reflections on foods I most associate with the different seasons. In addition, I pass on to you ideas of combinations of flavours, colours and textures that have worked well for me. Some choices you may find surprising, but I hope you will try them out.

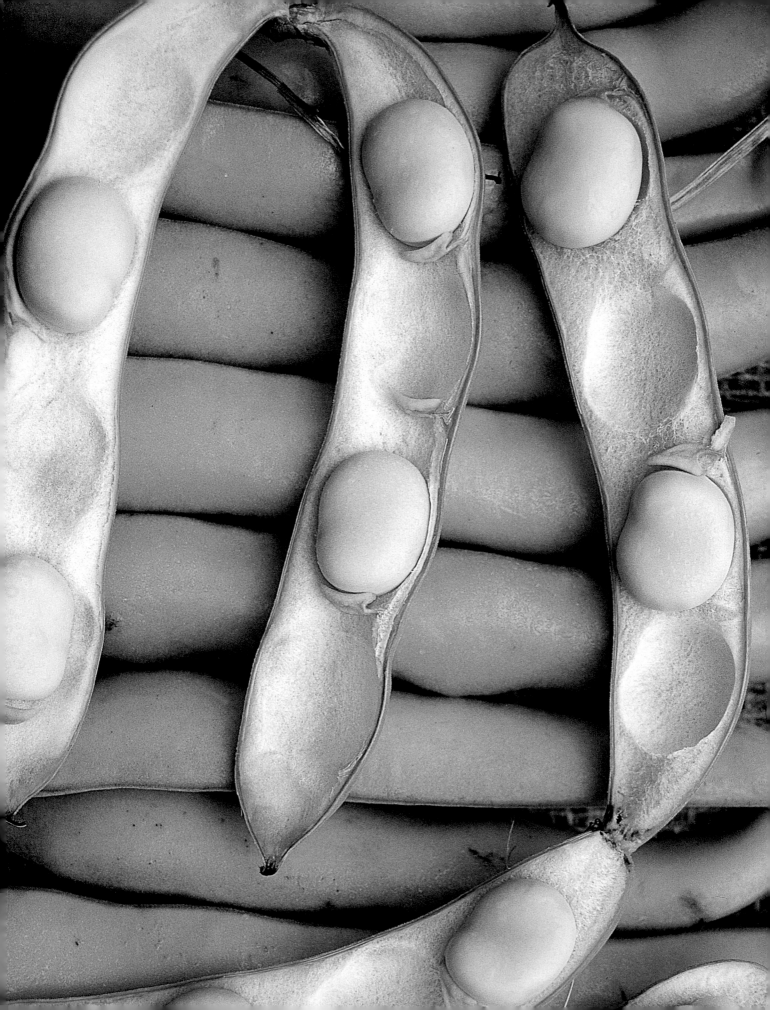

Seasonal Ingredients

Spring starts in my kitchen around March. The cold winds may still blow outside, but our spirits are lifted when the suppliers start to bring in treats from the warmer South of France. The lengthening of the days and the anticipation of the best of new season's produce perk us all up in the restaurant kitchens.

One of the first foods to appear are sweet **peas** in pods. They are so tender that you can just pop the pods and scoop out the tiny peas to eat raw. In France housewives like to cook the peas still in their pods because the pods are tender and full of flavour. I have a particular fondness for peas as they were the first vegetable I was allowed to prepare in a Paris kitchen, when I was promoted from sorbets on to 'veg' prep station. I had truly arrived! Peas are great with fish – I use the bigger ones puréed in a fish velouté. I am not wild about peas served cold, although I remember once enjoying a pea vinaigrette with cold lobster in Paris.

In the days of nouvelle cuisine many British chefs were accused of using baby **carrots** (and other baby veg) only as a garnish. The criticism haunted many of them, but now young carrots are back in favour, no longer on the back burner of fashion. Available for a good six months of the year, baby carrots first appear in spring, and we are able to get excellent locally grown carrots, straight and full of flavour. We just scrape and cook them lightly in butter with a splash of water. They're terrific with spring lamb, of course, but also try them with a braised fillet of cod, or cut them into thin julienne strips and serve them as a vegetable 'spaghetti'. Another idea is to cook them briefly and then souse in vinaigrette to serve cool.

To my mind, the Rolls Royce of spring vegetables are baby *fèves*, or **broad beans**. In France they are used as a luxurious garnish, or cooked in the same way as new peas – in the pods for a soup. My days at Jamin, Joël Robuchon's restaurant in Paris, saw me spending hours preparing *fèves* for the light, fantastic 'cappuccino' of *fèves* with baby lobster, one of the favourite spring starters on his menu. I've also eaten them as a warm salad with grilled cuttlefish. *Fèves* have a lovely earthy taste, and are good in many country-style dishes, such as with potato gnocchi or a salad with ricotta. Peas and *fèves* together make a good plateful, complementing each other in every way. Whilst one is sweet and tender, the other is fuller and more 'meaty' in texture. They work nicely as a twosome.

In top kitchens, **baby leaf spinach** now enjoys a designer-label status, but many trainee chefs make the mistake of boiling and squeezing the life out of the young delicate leaves. If my young commis want to please me, they just check for bruised leaves and stray weeds. When it comes to baby leaf spinach there are lots of don'ts: don't pinch off the stalks, don't wash roughly, don't crush in a spinner, don't boil smothered in water and, please, don't ever squeeze or chop the wilted leaves. The best of the best baby leaf spinach comes to us in the spring. We dress it simply in vinaigrette or cook it just with a tablespoon of water and a knob of butter. Sometimes it is so delicate that we simply put a small mound of fresh leaves straight on to a piping hot plate. They wilt instantly and need no further cooking.

A vegetable that is featuring more in my cooking is **pak choi**, which is a pretty Chinese cabbage with stems that look like Swiss chard and a flavour that is a glorious blend of spinach and artichokes. Our supplies come in at the end of spring and last well into midsummer. We cook the baby-size ones whole, allowing one per portion. They make a great presentation vegetable with roasted poussins, grilled John Dory or poached salmon. Pak choi is also ideal for stir-frying, as it cooks in seconds in a hot wok.

If *fèves* are the Rolls Royce of spring ingredients, then I'd describe **white asparagus** as a Ferrari on a test drive because it disappears so fast. Even white truffles have a longer season. I get really excited when it comes into the kitchens. The pearly-white cigar shapes have a gentle delicate flavour, much kinder on the palate than the more robust green asparagus. The stalks need just a little peeling. We always serve white asparagus as whole spears, often simply dressed in vinaigrette. The Americans are mad for it, and the French adore it with chicken (*poulet de Bresse*, of course) and some sautéed morels.

In season for much longer than white, **green asparagus** is particularly good as a garnish for main dishes. The stalks are often woodier than white spears, because they have a lower water content, so we peel almost the whole length, to nearer the tips. Our usual preparation is to blanch and refresh them, and then reheat in a little buttery water just before serving.

Two other varieties are the rare, pencil-thin wild asparagus and the stunningly pretty water asparagus, which is a delicate spring green with tips like baby sheaves of wheat. It's wonderful with fish dishes.

Root and tuber vegetables have a special place in our culinary repertoire. Up amongst the most favoured are **Jerusalem artichokes**, which, although available year round, we particularly enjoy using in early spring. Despite the name, they are not botanically related to globe artichokes, and they have nothing to do with the Holy city. It seems that the name is somehow derived from the Italian for sunflower (*girasole*), which is what they were called when they were introduced to Europe from North America. Both Jerusalem and globe artichokes were popularised in Europe by the French, who still use them in many different ways. Jerusalem artichokes need very little peeling (which is a good thing as they are knobbly, like a juicy root of fresh ginger) and have a rich velvety texture when cooked. We take advantage of this and use them to make sublimely smooth soups. Blanched and then sautéed in a little butter, the roots colour up beautifully.

Spring marks the arrival of, for me at any rate, the ultimate mushroom – the **morel**. I must have expensive tastes because my favourite ingredients (white truffles, white asparagus and morels) all have a very short season and resist fruitful cultivation, no matter how hard clever gardeners try. Fresh morels are around for just four to six weeks. They have the strangest shape and look like spongy, brown woolly hats. Morels are quite tricky to clean and need light scrubbing (like white truffles) and quick rinsing. We stuff the larger ones with a chicken mousse and use the smaller ones in sauces. Needless to say, I do enjoy eating them with spears of white asparagus, simply dressed with vinaigrette or melted butter.

During March and April, my supplier comes back from Italy with new season's **garlic**, which he gets from the mountainous terrain in the north. Not to be confused with wild garlic, these have smaller heads than normal garlic and taste sweeter. But they still have an overpowering pungency, which can kill other flavours in a dish. You can tame this by blanching the cloves several times in boiling water. The leaves of new season's garlic, which look a little like mint leaves, can be shredded to serve in risottos, or in dishes of beef, lamb or robust fish such as halibut. I like to confit garlic cloves, unpeeled, in goose fat, then fry them until the skins become nice and crispy.

We use a lot of **parsley**, both curly and flat-leaf. Curly-leaf has a very pronounced flavour, which is mellowed by blanching in boiling water. This intensifies the glorious dark green colour too. Once the blanched parsley is refreshed in iced water, we squeeze it dry and then purée. This parsley purée is mixed into creamy potato, whisked into sauces for fish and oysters, and even used as a light thickener. Flat-leaf parsley is ideal for garnishing, as it has a pleasant cleansing effect on the palate. It should not be chopped too fine as it bruises easily.

We also serve it with sardines tossed in vinaigrette, and we deep-fry sprigs of parsley to use as a fish garnish.

Chefs are sometimes accused of popularising cod so much that stocks are threatened by demand. Well, whilst I love cooking cod, I also enjoy other white fish. One is **whiting** (it's my Mum's favourite, popular in Scotland). Flaky and full of flavour, it has the strength of cod with a slightly softer flesh, making it brilliant for *a brandade*. Whiting is at its best in spring and quite easy to buy. Although the flesh is quite soft, it is not at all watery. I'd better say no more or whiting too will become popular and the price will start to creep up.

Have you noticed that **spring chickens** have become poussins? I suspect it has something to do with EU legislation, and that the name has been changed because they are available all year round. (The same thing has happened to spring onions, which are now called 'salad' onions.) For me, baby-size chickens will always be just right for light spring menus, so I'll stick to the original name. Supplies of spring chickens almost disappeared about ten years ago, but now they are fairly easy to get. We find people prefer to eat them at lunchtime, but not dinner, possibly because they seem lighter. My favoured cooking method is what the French called *poché-grillé* – we poach the birds whole in broth to par-cook them, then remove the breasts and legs and pan-roast them. That way the meat remains succulent and the flavour is enhanced by browning in a hot pan.

When it comes to meat cookery, spring is the season for new **lamb**. Somehow, heavier meats such as beef, game and, to a certain extent, pork seem

not quite appropriate for this time of year, while lamb appeals. It is tender, sweet and delicate in flavour, and the outside cooks in next to no time to a wonderful rich, caramelised, almost barbecue flavour. To my mind, almost all the best lamb is British. Our supplies come from a number of areas, depending on the season. I prefer Scottish and Welsh lamb in spring and, when possible, use milk-fed lamb. During the autumn, I like to get in lamb from the Pyrenees, where it is reared almost completely wild; later on in the season it takes on a more gamey flavour, like wild boar. Lamb is the most versatile of all meats. We use the little legs, cannons from the saddle (especially popular with our lady customers) and neck cutlets, and also the shanks for braising.

I have to confess, I'm a **Granny Smith** man because it is such a well-balanced apple – sweet and sharp with a firm juicy texture – and it is as good raw as cooked. We use it for many desserts – in iced parfaits, in fruit salads and as a sweet *jus* for our hallmark dessert, crème brûlée, by crushing the apple flesh at the last moment to make a simple sauce. And that's not all. Sliced wafer thin, dipped in stock syrup and then dried overnight, Granny Smiths make excellent (fat-free) *tuile* biscuits. You can't get a more versatile ingredient!

In late spring, small fragrant **apricots** with blushed pink skins begin to feature on our supplier's list. The apricots come from France and Spain, two countries that offer a number of wonderful recipes for this amazingly versatile fruit. We use it in both savoury dishes and in desserts. In my early days at the Aubergine, we had a pork dish with

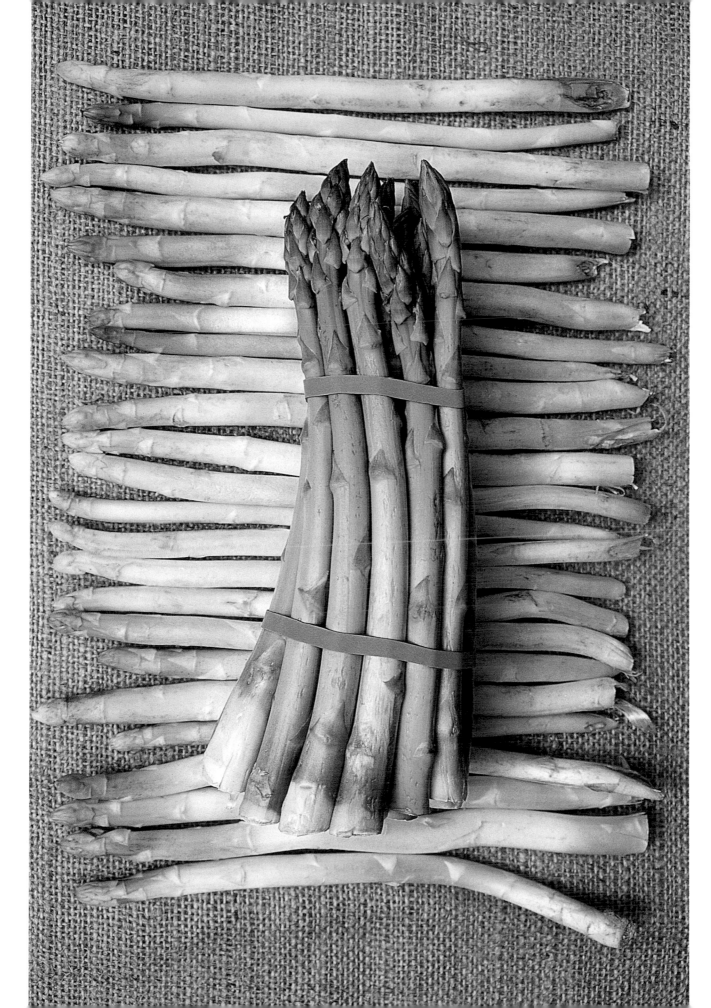

stuffed apricots on the menu, which won many fans. Clafoutis with baby apricots is a light easy pudding, or the fruits can be poached in a little cinnamon- and anise-scented syrup to serve with creamy rice pudding. The supply of small apricots lasts until the start of summer, when larger fruits arrive. Out of season, we use half-dried French apricots (what the French call *mi-cuit*) that need no pre-soaking. They are brilliant for jams.

The exotic fragrance of **mangoes** is simply wonderful. When buying, don't choose a mango that is too ripe – you need an edge of sharpness to balance the luscious sweetness. For savoury cooking, buy fruits that are hard and slightly acidic. Match them with sweet seafood or with chargrilled chicken or pork and a hint of aromatic curry spices. Under-ripe mangoes also make good relishes and chutneys. In the dessert menu, mangoes go well with butterscotch flavours, but my ultimate favourite 'marriage' has to be with coffee and cream, which we use in a sweet ravioli recipe. For this, peel a large, firm mango and cut wafer-thin slices. Soak them in stock syrup for a couple of hours to soften, then drain and pat dry. Make a filling from seriously strong espresso coffee, thick crème fraîche and softly whipped double cream, sweetening slightly. Scoop this into balls and lay between the sheets of softened mango.

I could wax lyrical about **rhubarb**. In spring we get tender, day-glo pink stalks, which are sometimes called 'forced' rhubarb because they are grown in hothouses or covered with tall pots (this makes them grow straight and tall). Champagne rhubarb is the most tender and sweet. We can generally get

rhubarb all year round, from either Kent or Holland, so when one supply is out, the other is in. Until the late 1940s this plant was classified as a vegetable, but it is now called a fruit. I use it as both. As a vegetable, we fry it and mix with choucroute, or use it to make a fantastic sauce for fish and lobster (this is quite a talking point at any dinner party) – sauté the chopped rhubarb in a little butter with salt and sugar, simmer gently in Vegetable nage (page 184) to a purée, then mix with some vinaigrette. Another savoury idea is to sauté rhubarb in butter, then deglaze with grenadine syrup and serve as a quick relish for foie gras or pan-fried liver. For me, the nicest sweet way to cook rhubarb is roasted with sugar, butter and vanilla, to serve with crème brûlée.

Summer begins around mid-May for me. In fact, by the third week of May I'm into the swing, because we are sited next to the Chelsea Flower Show and that, as every devotee of the social scene will tell you, is very definitely the start of the summer season. Lunch during Chelsea week is unbelievably manic, but we are graced with some very elegant guests – and lovely hats!

Let's start with **tomatoes**, which are full of tremendous flavour from all the early summer heat. We use mainly plum tomatoes (the best come from Italy) and home-grown cherry tomatoes on the vine. We like to stuff plum tomatoes with finely chopped ratatouille to serve alongside grilled fish such as red mullet, or pan-fried cannons of baby lamb. As a young commis chef in Paris, I remember being gobsmacked by one of Guy Savoy's starters – plum tomato halves filled with shredded braised oxtail and then gratinéed. It was perfection, the sharp, fruity tomato cutting the incredible richness of the oxtail.

Cherry tomatoes have made a great difference to our cooking. Not only do they have an excellent flavour, but also the wonderful red of their skins means we seldom have to add any tomato purée to a stock or stew to pump up the colour. Cherry tomatoes make great soups, delicious with thin floats of mozzarella *di bufala*, as well as a punchy gazpacho sauce and a tomato vinaigrette.

For a clever garnish, you might want to try making tomato *tuiles* or 'crisps'. It's really easy, but you do need to use an oven that has a very low setting – almost a plate-warming temperature. Failing that, you can prop open the oven door with a wooden spoon. All you do is thinly slice very firm, bright red plum or beef tomatoes with a serrated knife, lay the slices on a silicone cooking liner on a baking tray, and sprinkle with sea salt and black pepper. Then simply dry out in the low oven for a good few hours until the tomatoes are firm and you can peel them off the liner. Timing depends on your oven. In ours, it takes 12–16 hours on a pilot light (few domestic ovens have such things now). The first time you make them, start them in the morning and check after 4 hours, then thereafter every hour or so. Once they are dry, lay them on a wire rack to cool and crisp further.

Around Chelsea time we start to get in supplies of my favourite summer food, the kidney-shaped **Jersey Royal new potatoes**. I could happily sit and eat a bowl of them on their own, as they have so much flavour. From a cook's point of view, you can really do a lot with them because of their waxy texture. They make a good pomme purée, using the larger sizes – bake them on a bed of rock salt (to maintain the waxiness), peel while still warm (wearing rubber gloves, which we affectionately call our 'Marigolds') and then put through a potato ricer. We also crush boiled Jerseys against the side of a pan and mix in olive oil, chopped olives and tomatoes, to make *pommes écrasées*. And they are brilliant sautéed in olive oil or goose fat. The skins of Jersey Royals are so delicate that they only need to be lightly scrubbed if serving whole – plain boiled or warm in salads (for the simplest, just toss them whilst hot in some vinaigrette). A great potato salad is Jerseys mixed with a little home-made mayonnaise (thinned down slightly with cream or more vinaigrette) and chopped spring/salad onions and topped with chopped fresh parsley or chervil. Jersey Royals have such a short season – about six to eight weeks (they can't be grown anywhere else) – so we really make the most of them.

I don't know who first had the brilliant idea to try cooking with **courgette flowers**, but I am grateful for the source of inspiration. As an ingredient, they are truly versatile, with an enchanting, fragile beauty. We receive supplies of flowers with tiny wee vegetables, the length of my little finger, still attached. I know you cannot buy them easily, but home gardeners will find them simple to grow, so courgette flowers need not be thought of as elitist. In France, speciality growers insert thin plastic cups into the emerging flowers so the petals grow into a cup shape. This makes the mature flower the perfect shape for stuffing.

I use courgette flowers in two ways, always with the baby vegetable still attached. For the first, the flowers are filled with a light *farci* or stuffing, such as a mousse, a finely diced ratatouille or even a spicy cous cous, and then steamed over an aromatic simmering stock. I serve them with a delicate *jus* of Jerusalem artichokes or light velouté sauce. My

other favourite is to gently slit one side of the flower and open it up like a sheet of paper, then dip it into the lightest *beignet* or fritter batter and deep-fry for a minute or two in hot olive oil, to serve tempura-style with a little freshly made chilli jam.

Another summer favourite is wild **girolle** mushrooms (aka chanterelles), which we get mostly from France, although increasingly (I'm thrilled to say) from Scotland. Their warm golden-yellow colour adds a touch of luxury to our dishes. We tend to use the smaller ones for garnishing and serving with dishes. The larger ones are sautéed and served with mussels in a cream sauce, or made into a girolles *duxelles* to stir into fish veloutés. Girolles do need to be prepared carefully – thoroughly rinsed to remove all grit, and then left to dry completely.

After my time in Paris, I had a job cooking on a boat in the South of France, where I learnt about **black olives** firsthand. Whenever I could, I would make my way to the olive market in old Nice, to talk to the olive farmers, or should I say listen to them talking, because they were passionate about their fruits. In the restaurant we only use black olives from Nice. They are neat perfect fruits, and need very little added to them – no garlic, lemon or chilli. Finely chopped and mixed into a tapenade, we place them as quenelles on top of grilled salmon. We also sprinkle them on lamb niçoise or stir them into a fresh ratatouille. I find I can't stop myself from nibbling them on their own.

Another favourite from my time in the Mediterranean is fresh spriggy **thyme**, particularly lemon thyme. I use it in a variety of ways, all year round (there is no need to resort to using dried thyme

because it is generally easy to get hold of). In summer, thyme has an especially good zing, and a host of savoury and sweet dishes benefit from its presence. We pick off the tips of the sprigs, which we call 'flowers', and sprinkle them over lamb whilst it is roasting, over plump scallops and over sautéed new potatoes. We almost always use thyme in marinades and tie it up in bouquets garnis. We use it in sweet crème brûlées and even infused in the custard base for ice cream.

You can always tell when a food has become hip, because supermarkets start to sell their own versions. Some years ago it became fashionable to use edible flowers in salads, and for a time you could buy mixed salads with flowers. Fashions bloom and then fade, but we still enjoy using flowers in cooking, chiefly to infuse creamy mixtures such as custards or a rich chocolate ganache. The two flowers I enjoy using at the moment are jasmine and lavender. Both have light floral fragrances that add an inspired touch of mystery – even my regular diners can't guess the elegant flavour. We serve **jasmine** in a consommé, crystallise the dainty flowers for pastries, and use it to subtly enhance the flavours of a tea sorbet made with Earl Grey. While jasmine is used fresh, **lavender** flowers are best dried to concentrate the flavour and then rubbed to separate them from the stalks. We crush the flowers to mix (sparingly) into shortbreads or sprinkle them on to a rich bread dough before baking.

Two spices remind me of summer, even in the deepest winter – saffron and cinnamon. Both have a great depth of flavour and both need to be used

sparingly, otherwise your dish will suffer from overkill. Less is definitely more with them. It's important to ensure that **saffron** is very dry so the strands can be crushed into a powder with just fingers. We sprinkle saffron on the skin of fish such as red mullet, just a pinch per fish, then leave to marinate for 5 minutes or so. This allows the saffron flavour to permeate the flesh, and the skin cooks to a deep golden-red. We also use saffron in mussel soup, with leeks, and to give an exotic flavour and rich colour to pasta dough (first make a concentrated essence by crushing strands into a little boiling water, then shake a few drops into the dough as you knead it smooth). Saffron is classic in risottos and pilaffs (again, just a pinch or two), but have you ever tried it in ice cream? It's wonderful. Infuse strands in the cream and milk for the custard base before churning smooth.

You can make fantastic ice cream with **cinnamon** too, and it is wonderful in syrups for fruits such as apples and pears. But to my mind, the fruit that is made to be flattered by cinnamon is the black fig, which comes to us from Egypt in the late summer. We also use cinnamon, along with Chinese five-spice, in rich red wine sauces to serve with full-flavoured or firm-textured fish like brill or turbot.

Although the French boast about the freshness of Brittany **lobsters**, in the top Paris restaurants where I worked, the lobsters actually came from Scotland. Today, I always try to use lobsters that have been trapped in the clear loch-fed waters of the west of Scotland. If they are scarce, we use Canadian lobsters. When preparing lobsters a good rule to follow is: the more it costs, the less you need to do to it. One of my first signature dishes was roasted lobster with vanilla, simple but superb. In summer we poach lobsters in a court bouillon, then serve them on a spicy guacamole, with a fine clear tomato consommé. Lobsters are naturally vicious creatures and attack each other, pulling off claws if they can. As we often chop the meat for ravioli fillings, I buy what the trade calls 'cripples', which are minus one claw, occasionally two. The tail meat is still succulent and tasty, although the clawless lobster is a sorry sight.

I have a confession to make: I judge the ability of any new commis chef who starts in my kitchen by the skill he or she displays in opening the wonderful **scallops** delivered to our kitchens each day. Such beautiful food is pricey, and we cannot afford to make mistakes. We take only hand-dived scallops from the west of Scotland. They are delivered so fresh, they pulsate as we open them. This is not an easy task, as the shells are clamped very tightly shut. I tell new recruits that the secret is to be very cunning. It's man against muscle. Stick the tip of the knife only into the hinge and sever the muscle that holds both shells together. Once this is done you can feel the scallop relax, and the two shells can be prised open. Then put the knife tip under the scallop and its frilly skirt in the rounded shell and gently ease it all away, including the coral. (We don't use the corals, except to sometimes dry them out in a low oven overnight, then grind to a fine powder, for flavouring risottos or using in sauces.)

Scallops come in various sizes. Ours generally weigh in at around 50g after cleaning, without the corals. Much bigger than this, they hold too much water and

can be tough. The very freshest scallops are used raw, chopped into a *tartare*. My favourite way of cooking scallops is dusted with spices and sautéed, then tossed with baby new potatoes to make a warm salad.

The smaller queen scallops are ideal for risottos and mixed salads. They are a bit of a pain to open, but we find a butter knife helps with the shell and a teaspoon with detaching the scallop. Reared in warmer waters than 'king' scallops, the queens have a slightly sweeter flavour.

Fishing has been one of my great passions ever since I was a small boy, when my father would take my brother and me up to the Scottish lochs to fish. In early summer I itch to find time to catch **wild salmon** as they return to their spawning patches on the River Dee. After an incredible swim of thousands of miles, the flesh of these magnificent fish is muscular, full of flavour and a rich dark pink from their natural diet. Their tails and fins have an incredible span when compared to their less fortunate farmed kith and kin, and the heads taper to a pronounced hook nose, which they use to burrow under pebbles and rocks seeking food and shelter. Modern-day fishermen have the benefit of sophisticated underwater photo technology, which can chart the progress and size of the salmon as they swim home. And that is wonderful to watch.

Such perfect natural food needs very little embellishment from me – just neat trimming and simple grilling or pan-frying, 95 per cent of the time on the skin side, which should cook to an appetising crispness. Wild salmon and cod are the only fish I season a good 20 minutes ahead of time, to draw moisture from the

skin and enhance the flavour just a tad. Sometimes, I score the skin and spike it with tips of thyme sprigs, then rub the skin with olive oil.

I have quite a fondness for good **caviar** (I'm sure that comes as no surprise). My favourite is known as 'golden caviar', from the albino Caraburun sturgeon. In the restaurant we use mainly Osietra, with its firm texture and nutty flavour, and Sevruga, which is ideal for sauces and garnishes. It takes several years for a sturgeon to reach the size when the eggs are ideal for caviar, which is one reason it is so expensive. It is not always easy to get good value for money when buying caviar, and, although sold packed in cans, the quality can vary enormously. The eggs can be bruised or oily or the flavour can taste flat.

The best way of ensuring the best quality is to buy from a good supplier. My favourite brand is Imperial Caviar UK, which is run by an Iranian friend, Ramin Rohgar. Much has been written about the poor quality control of certain caviar suppliers and the problems of overfishing (once caught, the fish cannot be returned to the sea to continue growing). The Iranians seem to have the better quality controls. Also, the sturgeons in the south of the Caspian Sea are larger and not subject to overfishing. Caviar features on our menus with poached lobster and folded into crème fraîche as a garnish. We also fold it into scrambled eggs and fish veloutés and mix it with sea urchin butter. But, so it is said, the best way of eating caviar is from a mother-of-pearl shell with a fine mother-of-pearl spoon.

Even in summer, many of our clients enjoy a nice piece of steak, often with a light sauce such as creamed parsley

purée and sautéed summer girolles. A favourite cut of mine is **ribeye of beef**. Popular for many years in Scotland, it is now appearing on menus 'down south'. It is just as good as fillet for tenderness with, I think, more flavour. It takes just minutes to cook on or off the bone (on the bone it is the classic T-bone steak). We buy ribeye in a large piece, wrap it tightly in cling film and refrigerate for a good 24 hours to 'set' the shape, before cutting it into even-size steaks.

Summer isn't summer without **peaches**. My favourite ones are the white-flesh varieties from Italy, which reach our suppliers from May onwards. Later on, firm and juicy yellow peaches appear. While there is little to beat a perfect fresh peach served simply sliced, peaches are a very versatile ingredient and we capitalise on this in our kitchen, for both sweet and savoury dishes. At the height of gluts, we make Kilner jars of peach chutney to serve as a relish with fresh foie gras, pâté and butter-roasted chicken, and with cheese and walnut bread. Pan-fried peaches glazed with sugar and vinegar are memorable with duck, goose or lamb.

One of my favourite ways of serving peaches is to marry the sweet succulent flesh with aromatic thyme, a herb that seems to cut the richness of the peach flavour and heighten the fruitiness. It's a combination that works well for peaches simply poached in a thyme-flavoured sugar syrup and for peaches served with a home-made thyme ice cream.

We also make light, crisp peach *tuiles*, by slicing just ripe and firm fruit wafer-thin, brushing with stock syrup and oven-drying for a few hours. To get the roof-tile shape, we press the dried slices over a rolling pin and leave them to crisp. Peach *tuiles* are a very pretty garnish for creamy puddings.

In mid- to late summer our supplies of **figs** come in from Italy. These beautiful plump, dark-skinned fruits with a downy surface and pert little hooked tips have quite a short season, so we use them every way we can. You have to judge the ripeness fairly exactly. If under-ripe, they leak a white milkiness; if too ripe, they become squashy. I love to roast them whole with a balsamic-flavoured caramel or simply with sugar, butter and cinnamon. They can be simmered into a chunky chutney, delicious with foie gras. We also slice firm fruits wafer-thin and dry them as *tuiles*. My latest creation is fig *carpaccio*, which is embarrassingly simple to make. Take firm fruit and peel thinly, removing the tips, then cut in half and scoop out the seeds. Lay the halves between large sheets of cling film and bat with a rolling pin until very thin. Don't whack too hard, just enough to flatten thinly and evenly. Then freeze and keep like this until ready to serve. Remove from the freezer, peel off the cling film and place directly on a large flat dinner plate. Top with a coarse pâté, or some heavenly slices of pan-fried foie gras. What more can I say?

In the early days of the Aubergine restaurant, we were very daring and gave our guests ripe fresh **cherries** nestled in bowls of crushed ice instead of petits fours. The idea went down a storm, as the juicy fruitiness cleared satiated palates perfectly. At the height of summer, we get luscious dark red cherries from Spain, and I really enjoy working my way through a pile of them. At other times of the year, growers in Italy, America, Chile and South Africa fly us in beautifully sweet fruits. Cherries are good in both sweet and savoury dishes. They make a classic partnership with duck breasts, and I enjoy them as a simple dessert with caramel and a balsamic sauce. You can use fresh cherries in a dessert soup too, as well as to make fresh cherry ice cream – stone and crush about 300g ripe cherries, then blend with a rich crème anglaise and churn in an ice cream machine. This refreshing ice cream is great with almondy biscuits.

I know **chocolate** is not a seasonal food, but I associate it with summer because I like to combine it with the heady fragrance of lavender flowers. Lavender is something we normally associate with bathing, not baking, but in parts of France where it grows in profusion, it is often sprinkled into bread doughs and used in sweet baking. I was introduced to the idea of combining chocolate and lavender by a talented French chocolatier whom I met whilst cooking as a guest chef at the Singapore Raffles. Such a 'marriage' of flavours isn't really surprising, of course – from the early days of chocolate-making in Europe, cooks have enhanced chocolate with flowery flavours. Examples are rose, as found in chocolate-coated Turkish delight bars, and violet, geranium and other flower creams in chocolate boxes. Dark, milk and white chocolate all benefit from the lavender connection. With white chocolate, we like to melt the chocolate slowly, even overnight, over a warm hot cupboard, with a healthy-sized sprig or two of lavender flowerheads to give their perfume. The next day the lavender is strained or spooned out, leaving its flowery fragrance in the chocolate.

Autumn is a favourite season, but then I don't enjoy too much summer heat. In fact, when the days begin to shorten and we wake to an autumnal nip in the air, I do feel a tinge of relief. And excitement too, because with autumn comes the promise of bountiful harvests of fruits and vegetables at their best.

Of all the leafy vegetables that pass through my kitchen, I suppose **sorrel** is one of the most tricky to handle. The peppery astringent taste is terrific in lifting the flavour of fish dishes (especially poached salmon), soups and salads, but knowing when to add it is the key to success. If added too soon, the leaves wilt to a slimy dull green, so it is best to put it in at the last minute. Cooks sometimes add a handful of baby spinach leaves to a sorrel dish to enhance the colour, but I find this unnecessary if you leave it until the last moment. If you grow sorrel, pick the leaves just before you need them. The ideal size for flavour is about the length of a large bay leaf. Peel the fine fibres from the stalk, then shred the leaves. They are delicate and bruise easily, even more so than basil, so always use the sharpest knife you can.

I'm really fortunate in having had a number of proud moments in my career. One of the highlights of the summer of 1999 was cooking a celebration lunch for the opening of the Scottish Parliament at Kincardine House. But there was another memorable event that day. It was my first taste of spanking fresh **spinach** picked barely a few minutes before and brought into the kitchen by the gardener himself. Where would we be now without spinach in the kitchen? Modern market gardening and transport have made this wonderful vegetable indispensable. But like sorrel, it must not be overcooked and is best added at the last minute. In the autumn, spinach leaves are larger but still wonderfully tender, and they can be used for creamed soups and for serving under medallions of fish or pink meat. Blanch the leaves for a few seconds in boiling water, then immediately drain and refresh in a bowl of iced water. Press out the excess water, then reheat at the last minute with a knob of butter.

The last few years have seen the popularising of many vegetables that can now be easily grown under cover, including many exotics. One of the nicest is the ragged-leaf **wild rocket**, which to the untrained eye looks like a weed. More peppery and textured than the smoother, dark green rocket, wild rocket has a lot more uses than being tossed in a salad or used as a rustic garnish. The flavour is brilliant with full-flavoured cheeses such as Parmesan and tangy goat's cheese. Mixed with fresh goat's cheese and vinaigrette it makes a wonderful filling for home-made ravioli. I also like it roughly chopped and tossed into risottos at the last moment.

No offence, but **celeriac** must be the ugliest vegetable around. Maybe that's why it is so underrated. I suppose it could be described as the Cyrano de Bergerac of the kitchen – ugly on the outside, but wonderful within. It's delicious as a purée, brilliant in soups, good deep-fried as vegetable chips or grated raw as a salad, and perfect cooked fondant-style (sautéed first and then simmered in stock). In the autumn I like a truly decadent treat of creamed celeriac topped with shavings of Périgord truffle. Sometimes as an *amuse-gueule*, we serve a tiny salad of shaved apple and celeriac bound in truffle vinaigrette. Celeriac is so versatile a vegetable, I really do enjoy cooking with it.

Looking a lot like chubby grubs, **crosnes** (see photograph on page 26) look and taste like a cross between globe artichokes and salsify, although they are completely unrelated. They were imported to France from China in the nineteenth century and grown in a village called Crosnes, from which they took their name (they're also called Chinese or Japanese artichokes). We treat them in a similar way to Jerusalem artichokes – cooked and then tossed in brown butter with chopped parsley and lemon juice. They're terrific with pigeon and with full-flavoured fish.

A truly versatile vegetable, **cauliflower** is good whatever way you want to use it. It does, however, have a downside, which is the smell if you overcook it even by a few minutes. I think that is what puts some people off eating it. My hint to lessen the smell (apart from watch the clock) is to simmer the florets in a mixture of water and milk. In the restaurant, we use only the actual florets, without any stalk, although at home you might like to trim them longer. Cauliflower is tremendous with fish, especially sweet scallops. We have one recipe where baby-size florets are dipped in a *beignet* batter

and fried as fritters. We also slice large florets thinly, season them with curry spices, salt and pepper, and then fry them in olive oil until beautifully caramelised. When cooled to room temperature, we serve them with a simple dressing of puréed raisins, capers and water.

Another vegetable we put on for our autumn menus is **fennel**. I prefer to use baby fennel – the little hearts look like crab claws and, appropriately, are brilliant served with all kinds of fish dishes. I like the baby vegetables because they are very tender yet still possess a full aniseed flavour. Older fennel bulbs need to be peeled of the stringy outside fibres. Fennel is a popular Mediterranean vegetable, especially in the South of France. In Tunisia and Morocco you see carts piled high with crisp fennel bulbs, to be served no doubt alongside spicy lamb dishes and chargrilled chicken and fish. We like to top and tail baby fennel bulbs, then cook them whole in olive oil until lightly coloured.

The **aubergine** holds a special place in my heart. A few days before opening my first restaurant in Park Walk, London, we still hadn't thought of a name, or rather agreed on one. In a flash it came to me – the Aubergine, and so it came to pass. You can stuff aubergines, cube and stew them, even fry thinly as crisps, and use in almost anything from canapés to main courses. And this vegetable can get a cook out of trouble when faced with having to prepare a hearty dish for non-meat eaters. The only thing you cannot do is eat aubergines raw. If you intend roasting, stewing or grilling them, they do not need to be salted first (we call this dégorging), but if you want to fry them, it is best to draw out excess moisture first.

Sprinkle lightly with fine sea salt and drain in a colander for 20 minutes. Then rinse well and pat dry.

Aubergines can absorb a lot of oil, if you let them. To avoid this, I toss them first in oil, then brown them in a stinking hot, dry pan. To make a creamy purée, we halve the aubergines, slash the flesh a few times, brush both sides with olive oil, season and sandwich back together with slivers of garlic and sprigs of fresh rosemary inside. Wrapped in foil and baked in a hot oven, they take about 40 minutes for the flesh to soften enough to scoop out and purée. But we haven't finished yet. The purée is heated in a dry frying pan until reduced down a little, to drive off excess moisture, then it is mixed with finely chopped tomatoes, fresh coriander, extra virgin olive oil and seasoning, to make a sublime aubergine caviar – the basis for many of my early hallmark dishes.

One of my most fraught moments during the preparation of the World Cup Dinner for over 700 people in July 1998, at Versailles in Paris, was the preparation of a garnish of deep-fried courgette leaves. These had to be dipped in a light batter, fried and then pressed between two sheets of paper to flatten. I'm happy to say that we did manage to produce delicate, gossamer-thin leaves that looked fantastic. And this does nicely illustrate how versatile the courgette is as a food plant. In the early autumn it is at its best, and you can use the flowers, leaves and, of course, the gourd itself as a vegetable. Courgettes contain a lot of water, so suit light cooking. We never boil them, preferring to slice them thinly and then sauté in a little olive oil, or souse in a vinaigrette. And, of course, they're a

classic partner for aubergines in ratatouille. Try this idea for a starter, following the recipe for Tomato and Parmesan gratinée tarts on page 62, substituting courgettes for the tomatoes. After baking the pastry bases, spread with a little tapenade and arrange thinly sliced, sautéed courgettes over this. Top each tart with a thin slice of seared fresh tuna.

Perhaps because the UK is an island (and proud of it), we sometimes close our minds to foods that we think of as a bit 'foreign'. One of these is pumpkin – for a long time we have only associated it with Hallowe'en. Our shops have pumpkins in stock for about a fortnight at the end of October and then bang, they disappear almost overnight. What do people do with all that lovely flesh they've scraped out when making the jack o'lanterns, I wonder? Slowly, we are realising just how versatile pumpkin is, and the fact that there are several varieties. In the restaurant we like to use the pale green pumpkin with ridges, popular in France and with West Indian cooks. You don't have to buy a whole one, just a wedge or two will do nicely. And far from being in season just for a few weeks, you'll find pumpkins on sale in markets during the autumn and well into winter. We make a smooth golden soup with pumpkin, served with spicy fried scallops, and also use it as a ravioli filling. To thicken the flesh for the filling, after cooking we put it in a jelly bag and leave to drain overnight. Pumpkin makes a good simple purée to serve with rich meats such as venison or game, and 'marries' well with smoky pancetta and punchy Parmesan cheese. It has its sweet uses too. I love pumpkin with the Italian mostarda di fruta, and in a pumpkin and

frangipane flan, which I ate when I was a young chef in Paris.

No piece on autumn foods could appear without a good discourse on wild mushrooms. We always look forward to the boxes of fascinating fungi our suppliers bring in at this time of year. The tiny Smartie-size mousserons may look dainty, but they pack a lot of flavour. Unfortunately, they are quite fiddly to clean. We use them in soups, especially with mussels, and also serve them along with globe artichokes as a garnish vegetable for veal and pigeon. Another favourite is ceps – sometimes as much as 10 kilos a day of fresh ceps will pass through the kitchen, to be sautéed, confit, roasted or packed in jars with olive oil. We even hang them to dry until brittle, then grind them to a fine powder to scatter over risottos and fillets of sea bass or use as a flavouring for a clear consommé. Possibly the ugliest wild mushrooms, trompettes des morts look dark and sinister, but I love to serve them in warm salads or with roasted fillets of turbot. Occasionally, when we can get them, we put blewits on the menu. I call them the acid-house mushroom, because they look like drop-outs from a rave party. Their flesh is quite bitter, so we counter this by making sure they are well and truly sautéed, even to the point of overcooking. Then we stir in a spoonful of confit of sweet shallots to temper the flavour.

Hardly a day goes by when we don't have langoustines, also called Dublin Bay prawns, on the menu. They are indispensable as a fine food and have so many uses. Our langoustines come to us from the west of Scotland. They are

roasting, and, for a really strong colour, sometimes dip them into green lobster coral, which cooks to a vibrant pink.

I associate **mussels** with my first serious telling-off as a young chef in Paris. You see, in French restaurants, the hygiene regulations regarding mussels are very strict, and each chef who opens up a sack must pin the identifying tag to a board. Then, in the unlikely event of food poisoning, the source of supply can be traced back. As the young 'rosbif' from England, I knew nothing of this and threw out the tag. Fortunately, I wasn't fluent in French then (I am now), so didn't quite understand the 'finer points' of the abuse hurled at me by chef. Ouch! Two better memories of mussels in France are baking them in the shell with brioche crumbs and Gruyère cheese, and the delightful style of matching mussels with mushrooms, which the French call *terre et mer* (earth and sea).

Throughout the summer and autumn months, we feature **red mullet** frequently on the menu. It is obligingly good both hot and cold. Most of my red mullet ideas come from my time in the Mediterranean – like serving crispy-skinned fillets topped with a fine black olive purée (we call this a tapenade, although I omit the usual anchovies as they are too overpowering), or placing them on cous cous scented with lemon grass. And, of course, red mullet is one of the essential fish for a classic bouillabaisse. This we serve with croûtes topped with the chopped and sautéed mullet liver mixed with olive purée. We also simply pan-fry fillets or souse them in a vinaigrette.

Red mullet is a shallow water fish, and our supplies come from Brixham in Devon or from the South of France. The

transported in aerated tanks, which makes them very frisky by the time we receive them. If you flick their tails they snap straight back, certainly a sign of being very much alive. We find they peel easier if blanched for a minute in boiling water, dropping just a dozen at a time into the water. Then, after peeling, we stack them in tight rows on trays and chill to firm the flesh. Their heads are full of

flavour, so we sauté them to use in a langoustine stock for sauces. The heads also contain a membrane that acts as a clarifying agent for stocks, just like the albumen in egg whites – after simmering we find the liquid has become naturally clear. Langoustines are popular as ravioli fillings, or sautéed to serve with salads or in soups. We often dust them with curry powder or crushed saffron before

skins are the great attraction for me, so delicate and pretty. The scales can be easily picked off with fingers (we do this inside large bin bags). To get a firmer grip when filleting, my chefs bend the fish in a slight curve before cutting down the backbone. It's a neat trick. The bones and heads make good fish stock.

For years, diced **monkfish** was passed off as 'scampi'. Now it occupies a supreme place in fish cuisine and, where once derided as tasteless and watery, it is now in danger of culinary overkill. Like cod, we are in danger of overfishing it. You see, monkfish is a deep water fish and so is difficult to farm. It takes many years for monkfish to grow to maturity, so replenishment of stocks is slow, and supply is now falling behind demand. It is the tails we eat – the heavy bony heads are discarded. (The livers are tasty and can be cooked to serve as a garnish.) There is only one central bone, or cartilage, with two fillets on each side. These have to be skinned and the grey membrane carefully removed because it can cause the flesh to curl unattractively during cooking. After filleting, we often roll the flesh tightly in cling film, to tighten and firm it. For a few months I was Pierre Koffman's head chef at Tante Claire (now the site of my restaurant), and I remember well a brilliant monkfish recipe he did – a fillet tunneled out and stuffed with a finely diced ratatouille, then wrapped in a whole flattened, scored squid to be pan-roasted. Sheer genius. He served that with a saffron-scented risotto.

Unlike monkfish, **rabbit** is not in short supply. The French and Italians have a particular fondness for it and cook it like chicken or lean tender pork, with fresh rosemary or thyme. And hip New Yorkers are taking to it in their chic upscale eateries. We Brits still associate rabbit with flopsy bunny (or field vermin), although it is beginning to feature on some restaurant menus. We use the shoulder meat for stews (*pot au feu*), terrines and pâtés, and roast the saddles and legs. The carcasses form the basis of a very good stock, which can then be used to make a setting-strength aspic jelly for pâtés *en gelée*. The legs and shoulders we also confit slowly in goose fat until the tender meat can be pulled into shreds and then mix it with vinaigrette. Rabbit is good with gnocchi and a light and creamy mustard sauce, and with a caramelised tart of chicory. And the best end can be served as tiny chops with the kidneys as a garnish.

Autumn is the time for game birds. The shooting seasons start in late summer, although some, such as pigeon, are on sale year round. I had my first hunting experience with Marco Pierre White. His aim was much surer than mine – not only did he bag his birds in flight, but also the ones I missed. Maybe I'll learn … We get many of our game birds from the Petworth Estate in West Sussex – pheasants, wild ducks, woodcocks and so on. We get **pigeons** in from Anjou where they are reared in the wild. Most of the time we use only the breasts of wild birds, although the legs can be carved off too. The carcasses make good stock. The breasts are nice served sliced in a warm salad, and we use them as part of a game terrine. Pigeon breasts are particularly delicious served with a soft swede purée and the little artichoke-flavoured crosnes. We often pan-fry **pheasant** breasts with fresh thyme or serve with a salad of apple and celeriac tossed with a walnut vinaigrette. Older birds are used in a fricassée with lentils. If the birds have been badly shot, we use the meat to make a sausage bound with foie gras. Little dark-fleshed **wild ducks**, or sarcelles, taste like a cross between woodcock and grouse, and a lot gamier than normal ducks. Their legs are tough and sinewy, so we use a part poaching, part grilling method of cooking. Because the breasts are lean, we cook them on the bone and serve them pink.

Perhaps the foods we associate most with autumn are apples and pears. We like **Cox's apples** for *tarte Tatin* Cox's make good tart fillings because they contain less water than other apple varieties. Their flavour is also brilliant in parfaits because it is so distinctive. We dry wafer-thin Cox's slices as chips or *tuiles*, to use as a decoration. Sometimes in the autumn we mix lightly poached apples with chopped prunes and serve topped with an apple gratinée.

The flavour of **pears** is beautifully rounded and needs little else in the way of flavouring. Comice, Williams' and Conference pears are all ideal for cooking, as long as they are slightly under-ripe and firm – too soft and they taste floury and have lost their edge of flavour. There are savoury uses for pears, such as in a fruit relish for foie gras (flavoured with a hint of saffron). For desserts, pears are great for poaching in a spiced red wine syrup to be served with a rich peppercorn-flavoured crème anglaise and, like apples, they make a good compote. Their flowery fragrance is also nicely complemented by a hint of lime. We also dry thin slices of pear, then sandwich them together with a cinnamon ice cream, standing them upright on a compote of pears in red wine.

Winter, surprisingly, can be a very good season for a variety of foods. Roots and brassicas are in prime condition, a lot of game is in high season, and fish from icy waters is plump and full of flavour. And now that air transport is so fast and efficient, we can obtain wonderful quality fresh fruits and vegetables from the southern hemisphere. So we can really have the best of both worlds.

Frosty, cold conditions may wilt some vegetables, but it seems to make certain hardy greens such as cabbage and sprouts more spriggy. My favourite cabbages are the Savoy and Chinese leaves. Obligingly, both remain crisp and fresh for several days in the fridge. The dark green, outer leaves of Savoy cabbage we use for wrapping up small, tightly packed balls of shredded braised oxtail or confit of duck. We also like to dry the large outer leaves, to use as a crisp garnish for sweetbreads. For this, the leaves are sautéed whole, then packed between metal baking sheets lined with non-stick baking parchment and baked at the lowest oven temperature for about 45 minutes. Chinese leaves are wonderful with braised and poached fish. We shred the leaves finely into julienne strips, sauté them in butter with tips of thyme and then ladle in a little chicken stock just to moisten. This can be done ahead for reheating at the last moment.

Another very good leafy-cum-stalk vegetable for the winter months is Swiss chard, which I like to call by its French name *blette*. The two parts are prepared separately, with the leafy tops treated like spinach and the ribbed stalks like celery. They often need a light peeling before being cut into bâtons and sautéed. Chard is good with game. I also like to serve it with roasted bass with a vanilla-flavoured butter sauce (one of my first hallmark dishes at the Aubergine).

The Scots are very partial to swedes – I have many happy memories of my Mum's buttery golden purée – and they are popular in many other parts of the world. In France, however, swedes and other root vegetables were traditionally fed to the pigs. We may laugh at this, but I dare say the French could wag their fingers at us about our attitudes to celeriac and beetroot. The lightly sweet, slightly musky flavour of swede suits game birds such as pan-fried pigeons and roast guinea fowl as well as full-flavoured fish – I once tried it very successfully with a fillet of zander, a pike-perch type of fish popular in Europe. We cook swede in buttery stock first, then blend it until smooth and return the purée to the heat to dry off a little. Swede has enough body to stand on its own as a purée and doesn't need any potato.

The strange-looking kohlrabi may be a subject of curiosity for many of us, but take my word for it – the flavour cannot be matched by any other root vegetable. It resembles a turnip, but is sweeter and more delicate. I think kohlrabi is best diced and sautéed in oil and butter before being braised with a little chicken stock until just tender. Like this it's good with light game, and it makes a light creamy soup too.

We tend to take large 'old' potatoes for granted, tossing big bags into the supermarket trolley without looking at the label. But if you take time to check the variety, you can select potatoes with a fine flavour or those suitable for particular uses such as roasting or baking. I think it's worth paying a few extra pennies per kilo for the best – after all, a good potato is still the best value food. King Edwards, Desirée and Maris Piper are the 'aristos' of the spud world, being good for all uses. If you want to make mind-blowing mash, try baking them first, unpeeled, on a bed of rock salt. When soft, halve, scoop out the flesh and mash until smooth. Mix in half whipped cream and a good knob of best butter, and season nicely too – bland mash is a big disappointment. I like to serve chunky chips with steak tartare and – another example of the humble potato becoming a gourmet's delight – I make a simple creamy potato soup very special by stirring in fine shreds of black truffle.

A winter vegetable appreciated by both French and British chefs is salsify. Home cooks are beginning to discover its joys too. The weird, dark, thin cigar-shaped roots do look a little uninviting, but peel them thinly and underneath you will find pale cream flesh that looks similar to white asparagus. Salsify has a tremendous flavour – robust and strong. Once peeled, it needs to be dunked into lemony water because it

browns quickly. After a blanch in boiling water, you can cut the stalks into thin lozenge shapes and sauté them in olive oil and butter until lightly browned. Salsify is fantastic with duck, veal and flat fish such as brill.

Although on sale almost all the year round, **leeks** are most associated with winter dishes. In fact, leeks are best in the winter, before the inner cores harden, and we don't waste any part of them. The large outer leaves have a number of uses in our kitchen. The tougher ones act as wraps for bouquets garnis, while large inner leaves are turned into an attractive garnish: we shred them very finely and deep-fry, then crisp up in a low oven, ruffling through the shreds as they dry out to make them a bit 'bouffant'. We confit bâtons of inner leek (and baby leeks too) in goose fat for about 8 minutes, then drain and grill until crispy on the outside. Leeks marry well with most other flavours, but I particularly like to sprinkle a pinch or two of crushed saffron strands over them as they braise in buttery stock or simmer in a leek soup. Whole baby leeks are great blanched and served with a lemon butter sauce.

If you are looking for unusual vegetable chips, then try leek leaves. Split open the white of a leek and cut the layers into large bite-size squares. Blanch to soften, then pat dry and brush each side with truffle oil. Dry them out in a very low oven until crisp. They'll be a sure talking point at any party, I promise.

Some vegetables have a foot in both camps – hot and cold. One of these is **chicory** (or endive, as the Continentals call it). Although most commonly used as a salad vegetable in the UK, in my kitchen we usually serve

them cooked. They are best caramelised first in hot oil with sugar, salt and a touch or two of Chinese five-spice. After this they can be moistened with fresh orange juice and a little chicken stock, covered with a butter paper and braised in a medium hot oven for about 15 minutes until tender but not soft. Braised chicory is great with fish, chicken and rabbit. I also like to make chicory 'fans' (make them like the fennel fans on page 108).

Where would any chef worth his or her salt be without **Puy lentils?** In France, where these lentils come from, they even have their own AOC. The uses for Puy lentils are almost endless. They're fantastic in soups, like our well-known cappuccino of lentils with langoustines; great mixed with a fine *brunoise* of carrots, celery and onions as a 'garnish' for lamb; and wonderful tossed with vinaigrette to serve with pigeon. Marcus Wareing, my head chef at Petrus, has an imaginative way of serving Puys with braised onion petals flavoured with truffle oil. We also use a fine purée of lentils as a thickener in soups and velouté sauces, although it does darken the colour somewhat. If you can't get Puy lentils, the larger greeny lentils from Canada are a reasonable substitute.

There is certainly an art to opening an **oyster**, and once you have mastered it you must then fine tune it with lots of practice! (The other two marks of a good chef are filleting a sea bass and turning an artichoke.) You must never try to open an oyster from the side, it must be from the hinge at the top. Wrap your hand in several layers of thick tea towel, and cup an oyster with the flat shell uppermost. Take a firm stubby knife with a good point (the classic oyster knife,

if possible) and stick it in firmly, but not violently, at the hinge end. Wiggle it a little from side to side, and you should suddenly feel a 'give' as the hinge muscle is cut. Push the knife tip in a bit further and twist to lift up the shell. Inside is the oyster and juice. Be sure to save the juice. Slip the knife under the oyster to release the muscle, and that's it. A good oyster-opener leaves no bits of shell inside, although a novice is excused the occasional bit. The essence of opening is not speed but care. If we cook oysters at all, we just poach them in their own juice with a little nage and a couple of whole star anise. The smoky aromatic flavours blend sublimely. Native oysters (or Belons) are in season during the winter. They are more tricky to open than the commonly available Pacific oysters with their craggy shells.

There are many fishes more often associated with winter than warmer days. The first that comes to mind for most people is **cod**. Maybe that's because roasted and served with creamy mash, it's the ultimate comfort food. I associate cod with winter because that is when I used to go line fishing for it off a western Scottish beach with my dad. I think we were entrants in the White Horse whisky fishing championships. Anyway, although it is a great feeling to catch a big fish, from a cooking point of view, any fish over 5 kilos will be too flaky to hold together in the pan. The flakes are just too mealy, although the flavour is still fantastic. Instead, in the kitchen we like to cook smaller codlings around the 1.5–2 kilo size. Once filleted, the best way to cook cod is skin side down in a really hot pan, so the skin sizzles and becomes very crispy. Then serve with a garlicky pomme

purée or a vinaigrette of Puy lentils. (Incidentally, when you cook cod skin, do check that the fine small scales have been rubbed off. It's not often the case.)

In today's quality restaurants, brill is becoming as popular as turbot. It's a strong fish, so can take a red wine marinade and full-bodied sauces made with chicken or veal stock, yet it still retains a fine tender texture when eaten. Brill are generally longer than turbots, but when they are small it is hard to tell them apart. If you buy a whole fish, turn it upside down and look for the 'oysters' by the jaw bone. Fillet them out with a sharp knife and pan-fry like scallops – they are a good cook's treat, or a garnish should you feel generous and want to share them. Brill bones make wonderful fish stock because they are quite gelatinous. Roast the brill bones first, as you would do meat bones, then cook in a red wine stock with strips of smoky bacon.

Red meats are a natural for winter dishes, and we are finding people are increasingly willing to try venison. Our venison is farmed on an estate in Aberdeenshire, where the deer are allowed to roam almost at will, so they are virtually free-range. The meat is hung for 2–3 weeks. After butchering, we marinate it in a neutral oil like groundnut with crushed juniper berries and fresh rosemary for a good 7 days. This opens up the muscle fibres and makes the meat really tender. We sometimes roast the loins and serve with rounds of fresh beetroot cooked fondant-style, in a little stock. Another favourite way of serving is with a garnish of chopped cabbage, turnip and carrot all braised together and then bound with a little cream. Slices of just pink venison are laid on top and nappéed

with a red wine sauce enriched with a bit of dark chocolate. The flavour intrigues our diners. A few fresh raspberries on top completes the elegant presentation.

Pork doesn't appear much on my menus, yet it is a meat that I think is perfect for serving home-cooked on chilly winter days. I love it with cabbage flavoured with a few pods of cardamom. If you find a butcher who still does his own cutting up, ask for the whole fillet of pork under the loin, the piggy equivalent of beef ribeye. The main way we use pork is pig's trotters. My restaurant is on the site of what was Pierre Koffman's renowned Tante Claire. As I was once Pierre's head chef, this is a significant honour for me. Pierre's genius gave London many great dishes, but perhaps his best known were *pieds de cochon*, or stuffed pig's trotters. His most famous was a stuffing of sweetbreads and morels. My recipe for pig's trotters in a thick, flavoursome braising liquid is a favourite staff lunch.

Another animal extremity that makes fine eating is oxtail. After an unnecessary (to my mind at least) ban of beef on the bone, we are now able to restore this classic casserole to its deserved pride of place on our winter menus. We stew oxtail gently in red wine with a mixture of root vegetables, stock and a hint of spice. When the meat is very tender, it is pulled into shreds and bound in a ball with thin *crepine* or set in a terrine to be served in slices with a salad of lentils in mustard vinaigrette. Butchers sell oxtails as sets, with the vertebrae cut neatly into discs and bound with string. For a simpler serving, you could simply cook them as a normal rich beef stew, but do try to take the time to remove the

meat from the bone before serving.

Two fruits brighten up the long winter days for me (not that we see much daylight in our kitchen). These are pineapples and citrus fruits. Large sweet pineapples come from the tropics and travel well. You can check their ripeness by pulling out a green leaf at the top – just a tug should do it. We use pineapple in *tarte Tatins*, compotes and sorbets, and to make terrific *tuiles*. For a light dessert, blend the flesh with a caramel sauce, and top with creamy yogurt and shavings of a fruit granita.

Oranges, lemons and limes are the fruits we most associate with winter, which is strange considering they don't grow in our cold climate. But they do travel and store well, and we are certainly grateful for them. Blood oranges and pink grapefruit are the two citrus fruits I like to feature when they come into season – blood oranges for their rich colour and startling flavour, and pink grapefruit because they break down into the prettiest little tear shapes. These we mix into a vinaigrette and serve with a warm salad of red mullet or poached Scottish lobster with fresh coriander.

One of our most refreshing desserts is a terrine of sliced citrus fruits served with a tangy lemon sorbet. We also soak thin slices of lemon in stock syrup to make a sweet confit, and press them on to fillets of fish or sweetbreads before pan-roasting and serving with harissa-flavoured cous cous. The same confit can be prepared with lime slices, and used to flavour pan-fried pigeon breasts. Limes also feature as the tangy flavour in guacamole and in honey syrups for poaching all kinds of fruit.

Soups

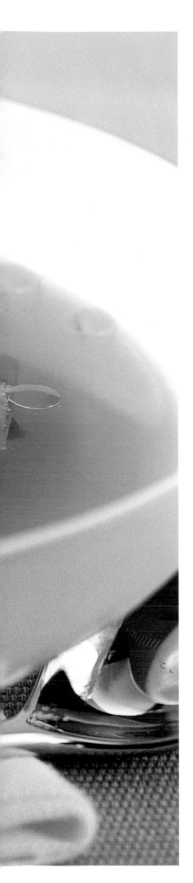

Light tomato broth with a paysanne of vegetables

This is a version of a tomato consommé we serve in the restaurant with baby lobster tails. As a chilled summer soup it is unsurpassed. I guarantee you will not taste such a full, fresh tomato flavour anywhere, yet it looks as clear and bright as a glass of sparkling wine. The dainty floating garnish flaunts the choicest summer vegetables. SERVES 4

2 large shallots, chopped

4 tablespoons olive oil, plus extra for serving

1kg ripe plum tomatoes, roughly chopped

2 cloves garlic, sliced

1 teaspoon fine sea salt

1 teaspoon sugar

1 teaspoon each chopped fresh basil,
   chervil and tarragon

4 free-range egg whites

¼ teaspoon each white peppercorns
   and black peppercorns

50g mangetout, trimmed

50g fine green beans, topped and tailed

about 20 asparagus tips

1 Sweat the shallots in 3 tablespoons of the oil for 3 minutes until softened, then stir in three-quarters of the chopped tomatoes, the garlic, sea salt, sugar and herbs. Cook over a medium heat for about 10 minutes, stirring occasionally, until a little pulpy.

2 Pour in 1 litre water and bring to the boil. Simmer for about 20 minutes, skimming the surface of any froth with a large spoon.

3 Line a colander with a large wet piece of muslin or thin clean tea towel and set over a basin. Pour the tomato liquid through the colander, pressing down on the debris with the back of a ladle. Chill the liquid by standing the basin in a bowl of iced water.

4 Whiz the remaining chopped tomatoes with the egg whites and peppercorns in a food processor. Tip into a large saucepan and add the strained tomato liquid.

5 Bring the contents of the pan slowly to the boil and simmer for 20 minutes. You should notice the liquid becoming crystal clear as it bubbles.

6 Rinse out the muslin or tea towel and place back in the colander set over a bowl. Slowly pour the liquid into the lined colander – it should run through beautifully clear. If it does not, slowly pour it back through the colander set over another bowl. Chill until ready to serve.

7 To make the garnish, cut the mangetout in diamonds. Heat the remaining tablespoon of oil in a small frying pan and gently fry the mangetout, beans and asparagus tips for about 3 minutes until just wilted. Drain on kitchen paper towel.

8 Scatter the mangetout, beans and asparagus into four large soup bowls. Pour over the clear broth. If you like, you can drizzle over some extra virgin olive oil, then serve straightaway.

Pepper and tomato soup with crab cocktail

A soup does not have to be brimming with liquid and a miscellany of floating diced solids. Sometimes I like to create a centrepiece of a mixture like this seafood cocktail and surround it with a light, flavoursome broth. Choose ripe, plum tomatoes for this recipe. If you wish to give the pepper more kick, grill or roast it first. Fresh crab is best, as it is less watery than frozen and has a sweeter flavour than canned. In the colder winter months you could use lobster meat instead of crab. **SERVES** 4

3 tablespoons olive oil, plus
   extra for drizzling
2 large red peppers, about 500g
   total weight, chopped
6 large, ripe plum tomatoes, about 500g
   total weight, chopped
4 shallots, chopped
about 12 leaves fresh basil
1 sprig fresh thyme
1 small bay leaf
800ml tomato juice
100ml double cream
250g fresh white crab meat

1 Granny Smith apple, peeled,
   cored and finely diced
1 baby Cos or romaine lettuce,
   finely shredded
1 ripe avocado
sea salt and freshly ground black pepper

Sauce
4–6 tablespoons Mayonnaise (page 184)
1 tablespoon tomato purée
a few drops of hot pepper sauce
juice of 1 lime

1 Heat the oil in a large saucepan, then add the peppers, tomatoes, shallots and herbs. Sauté gently for about 5 minutes, then stir, cover and leave to cook gently for 10 minutes.
2 Uncover, and remove the thyme and bay leaf. Stir in the tomato juice and cream, season well and allow to cool. Whiz in a food processor or blender until smooth and creamy, scraping down the sides once or twice. Rub through a sieve into a bowl, using the back of a ladle. Chill the soup for a good 2 hours.
3 Meanwhile, check the crab with a fork for any flecks of shell and cartilage, which can be so irritating to bite on in the middle of a dream dish. Put in a bowl with the apple and lettuce.
4 For the sauce, beat the mayonnaise with the tomato purée, pepper sauce, half the lime juice and some seasoning. Mix just enough into the crab to make a nice firm but moist mixture.
5 Crush the avocado with a fork. Add the remaining lime juice and some seasoning.
6 Check the soup for seasoning. (Chilled foods need more seasoning than hot ones.)
7 Set a plain scone cutter, about 5cm in diameter, in the middle of a wide soup bowl. Spoon a quarter of the avocado into the base of the cutter, then add a quarter of the crab mix over that. Finally, nappé the top of the crab with a little of the remaining cocktail sauce, and carefully lift off the cutter. Repeat with three other bowls.
8 Pour the soup around each crab cocktail, add a drizzle of oil if you like, and serve immediately.

Aubergine and pepper soup with sautéed cherry tomatoes

This chilled summer soup uses twice-roasted aubergines and peppers. It is an unusual recipe that bursts with Mediterranean flavour. Small servings could be given as a starter, or larger ones for a light main meal with warm French bread or ciabatta. **SERVES 6**

4 medium aubergines

leaves from 1 sprig fresh rosemary

1 tablespoon chopped garlic,
   preferably new season's

olive oil, for frying

2 large red peppers

2 large yellow peppers

1 shallot, chopped

2 sprigs fresh basil

1 tablespoon coarsegrain mustard

300ml Vegetable nage (page 184)
   or Light chicken stock (page 184)

about 250ml tomato juice (optional)

about 200g cherry tomatoes on the vine

sea salt and freshly ground black pepper

1 Preheat the oven to 190°C, Gas 5. Peel the skin from the aubergines in long strips using a swivel vegetable peeler, taking about 5mm of flesh still attached to the skin. Cut the skin into thin strips and then into small dice. Set aside.

2 Wrap the peeled aubergines in foil with the rosemary leaves and chopped garlic. Roast for about 45 minutes or until the flesh has completely broken down and softened. Save the cooking juices.

3 Heat about 2 tablespoons of olive oil in a large frying pan and, when hot, cook the soft aubergine flesh over a high heat to give it a slightly scorched flavour. Mix in the saved roasting juices and season. Remove from the pan and set aside to cool.

4 Stand the peppers upright on a board and cut the flesh from the central seed core and stalk. (This is a good tip – it stops the seeds flying everywhere.) Chop the pepper flesh.

5 Add another tablespoon or two of oil to the frying pan and, when hot, sauté the shallot until lightly coloured. Mix in the peppers and continue frying over a high heat for about 5 minutes. Mix in the basil and mustard, then the vegetable nage or stock. Bring to the boil and season, then simmer for 12–15 minutes. Remove from the heat and cool.

6 Discard the basil, then pour the pepper mixture into a food processor or blender. Add the aubergine and whiz until smooth and creamy. The soup will be quite thick. If you want it thinner, then gradually mix in tomato juice. Chill until ready to serve.

7 To prepare the garnish, heat a little oil in the frying pan and fry the reserved chopped aubergine skin until light and crisp. Take care not to overbrown. Drain on kitchen paper towel.

8 Add a tad more oil to the pan and heat it. Pull the tomatoes from the stalks and fry them, just to flavour the skin. They will go a bit squashy, which is fine. Drain on kitchen paper towel.

9 Check the seasoning of the soup – it should be quite pungent and full flavoured – then pour into four to six chilled bowls. Divide the sautéed cherry tomatoes among the bowls and scatter over the crispy aubergine flakes.

Chilled cucumber soup with ribbons of smoked wild salmon

Little demi-tasse cups of a light cucumber soup are frequently served in the restaurant as an amuse-gueule *– an appetite-teaser. The secret to the depth of flavour lies in the marinating and the use of my light fragrant vegetable nage. Don't serve too much – keep the delicacy intact. Some fine slices of smoked wild salmon (as made by the established East London firm, Forman's) contrast prettily with the pastel green soup.* **SERVES 4–6**

2 large cucumbers, washed and dried
2 tablespoons creamed horseradish
500ml Vegetable nage (page 184)
a small fistful of fresh mint stalks
200ml double cream
about 100g smoked wild salmon
sea salt and freshly ground black pepper

1 Cut off the ends of the cucumbers. Thinly slice them, complete with skin (which gives the soup its glorious colour). This can be done on a mandolin or using a slicer attachment on a food processor. Place in a large bowl.
2 Stir in the horseradish and vegetable nage with a little seasoning. Twist the mint stalks to release the flavour, then mix these in too. Cover and chill for 2 hours or so.
3 Remove the mint stalks, then whiz everything to a smooth purée in a food processor or blender. Pass the liquid through a fine sieve into a bowl, rubbing the pulp through with the back of a ladle. The soup should be quite thick. Whisk in the cream and check the seasoning – chilled soups should be well flavoured or they will disappoint.
4 Slice the salmon into thin strips and place in the centre of four to six soup bowls, depending on whether you want to serve a lot of soup or a daintier portion. Pour the chilled soup around and serve immediately.

Note Instead of smoked salmon, you could try a little shredded smoked eel.

Spring pea soup

This is a light creamy soup that has everything going for it – a tempting colour, velvety-smooth texture and a wonderful fresh flavour. Pea and bacon are a popular combination. I like to use bacon from Alsace, but another lightly smoked, dry-cure streaky bacon would be equally perfect.

SERVES 4

100g lightly smoked streaky bacon
  (preferably Alsace Ventrech), rind removed
2 shallots, sliced
2 tablespoons olive oil
400g fresh peas in pods, podded
2 tablespoons dry white wine
1 litre Light chicken stock (page 184)
  or Vegetable nage (page 184)
100ml double cream, plus a little extra to serve
sea salt and freshly ground black pepper

1 Reserve 4 rashers of bacon and chop the rest. Place the chopped bacon in a saucepan with the shallots and oil. Heat until sizzling, then sweat over a low heat for about 5 minutes.
2 Add the peas and cook for a further 2–3 minutes. Pour in the wine and cook until it has evaporated.
3 Stir in the stock or nage and 250ml of water, and bring to the boil. Season, and simmer for 15 minutes. Whiz in a food processor or blender until smooth, then pass through a fine sieve into a bowl, rubbing with the back of a ladle. Leave to cool and then refrigerate.
4 Meanwhile, grill the reserved bacon rashers until crispy. (In the restaurant we bake the rashers between two heavy baking sheets to keep them straight and flat, but you may prefer the crinkly look.) Drain well on kitchen paper towel so they aren't greasy. Keep warm.
5 When the soup is well chilled, check the seasoning and whisk in the cream. Season again. Serve in bowls with a little extra cream trickled on top and a floating bacon rasher.

Jerusalem artichoke soup with morels

Once regarded as a boring winter vegetable, Jerusalem artichokes are now enjoying a revival and are back in fashion. At New York's Daniel's Restaurant, they just scrub the roots rather than peeling them. You can do that for this soup, which will give it a rustic pale grey-beige colour. If peeled, the soup will be paler.

Fresh morels have a very short season, so you should try to make the most of them when they're available. We always prepare them a good hour before cooking, washing them very carefully – ours are grown in sand, and even a few grains can ruin this sublimely smooth soup – and then leaving them to dry. Out of season, you can use 50g dried morels, first rehydrating them in warm water. **SERVES 4**

150g small fresh morels

400g fresh Jerusalem artichokes

juice of 1 small lemon

3 tablespoons olive oil

2 shallots, chopped

100ml dry white wine

1 litre Light chicken stock (page 184)
  or Vegetable nage (page 184)

150ml double cream

25g butter

a little freshly grated nutmeg

sea salt and freshly ground black pepper

1 Cut the morels in half lengthways, then rinse well in cold running water to extract all the sand. Pat dry on kitchen paper towel and leave for 1 hour to dry completely.

2 Either scrub the artichokes or peel thinly with a swivel peeler. Fill a bowl with cold water and add the lemon juice. Cut each artichoke into slices and drop immediately into the acidulated water (this will stop them browning). Leave to soak for 5 minutes, then drain and pat dry.

3 Heat 2 tablespoons of the oil in a large saucepan and gently sauté the shallots for 5 minutes. Add the artichoke slices and cook for another 5 minutes.

4 Add the wine and cook until it has all evaporated. Pour in the stock or nage. Bring to the boil, season and simmer for 15 minutes or until the artichoke slices are softened.

5 Whiz in a food processor or blender, then pass through a sieve, rubbing with the back of a ladle. Return to the pan and mix in the cream. (At this point, you could chill and freeze the soup to serve later.) Heat until on the point of boiling, then set aside.

6 Heat the remaining oil with the butter in a frying pan and sauté the morels for about 5 minutes, stirring often. Season and sprinkle with a little freshly grated nutmeg. Drain on kitchen paper towel.

7 Reheat the soup, if necessary. Ladle into four warmed soup plates and scatter over the morels. Serve quickly. No garnish needed, save the morels – simple and sublime!

Asparagus soup with fresh cheese croûtes

The lightest of spring soups, this has dainty floats of chèvre and mascarpone croûtes made from a ficelle (thin baguette). The soup can be made ahead and then reheated to serve.
SERVES 4

500g fresh green asparagus
2 tablespoons olive oil
1 medium onion, finely chopped
1 small carrot, finely chopped
20g butter
2 sprigs fresh thyme
1 litre Light chicken stock (page 184)
  or Vegetable nage (page 184)
sea salt and freshly ground black pepper

To serve
1 ficelle (thin baguette)
2 cloves garlic, peeled
some light olive oil, for shallow frying
100g semi-soft chèvre, rind removed
1 tablespoon mascarpone

1 Trim the base of the asparagus spears, and use a swivel peeler to peel the skin from the stalks if a little tough. Cut off 12 tips about 5cm long. Chop the rest of the asparagus.
2 Heat the oil in a large saucepan and gently sauté the onion and carrot for about 5 minutes. Add the butter and, when melted, stir in the chopped asparagus and thyme sprigs. Sauté for 5 minutes, then cover and sweat over a low heat for a further 15 minutes until the asparagus is nicely softened, stirring occasionally.
3 Pour in the stock and add some seasoning. Bring to the boil, then cover and simmer for just 5 minutes – this keeps the flavour fresh. Check the texture of the asparagus stalks – they should be very tender. Remove the thyme sprigs.
4 Lift the vegetables into a food processor or blender using a slotted spoon, reserving the liquid in the pan. Whiz until creamy, slowly adding the liquid to the processor bowl. For a velvety texture, pass the purée through a sieve back into the saucepan, rubbing with the back of a ladle. Check the seasoning and set aside.
5 Blanch the reserved asparagus tips in boiling water for 2 minutes, then drain and plunge into a bowl of iced water. Drain again and set aside.
6 To make the croûtes, cut the ficelle into 1cm slices. Allow 2–3 slices per head. (You may not need all of the bread.) Rub the slices on both sides with the garlic. Heat a thin layer of oil in a frying pan and, when hot, cook until golden brown and crisp on both sides. Drain immediately on kitchen paper towel and cool.
7 Beat the chèvre with the mascarpone and season lightly. Spread in attractive swirls on the croûtes.
8 Reheat the soup, check the seasoning and pour into warmed soup bowls. Float the croûtes and asparagus tips on top and serve.

Spinach velouté soup with goat's cheese quenelles

Velvety-smooth, vibrant green and very simple – just the pure flavour of the vegetables topped with a light and silky cloud of goat's cheese and mascarpone. **SERVES 4**

400g fresh leaf spinach
2 tablespoons olive oil
1 medium potato, about 200g,
    peeled and thinly sliced
a little freshly grated nutmeg
100g fresh soft goat's cheese
40g mascarpone
1 tablespoon chopped fresh chives
150ml double cream
sea salt and freshly ground black pepper

1 Pick over the spinach, discarding any large, tough stalks and bruised leaves. Wash the remainder well in two changes of cold water, then shake off the excess water.

2 Heat the oil in a large saucepan and sauté the potato for about 5 minutes until soft. Add the spinach and stir it over the heat until well wilted.

3 Add 1 litre of water plus seasoning to taste and a little grated nutmeg. Bring to the boil, stirring. Partly cover the pan and simmer for about 15 minutes, stirring once or twice.

4 Meanwhile, beat the goat's cheese and mascarpone together until softly stiff, and fold in the chives. Season if you want to. I don't. Set aside.

5 Ladle the soup into a food processor or blender and whiz until smooth. Pass through a sieve back into the saucepan, rubbing with the back of a ladle.

6 Stir in the cream and slowly bring to the boil. Taste and adjust the seasoning. Simmer for a minute or two.

7 Ladle the soup into warmed bowls. Shape the goat's cheese mixture into quenelles, or just carefully drop spoonfuls in the centre of the soup, and serve immediately.

Variation For a special occasion, I sometimes make this soup with oysters. I shuck eight, saving all the juices. The four largest oysters I poach gently in the juices for a minute or two, then drain, reserving the juices. The other four I whiz in the food processor with the spinach and potato mixture. All saved oyster juices are added at this point. When the soup is served, I place a poached oyster in the centre of each bowl and spoon the goat's cheese mix on top.

Cauliflower and sorrel soup

A simple cream soup, this is ideal for when the nights start to draw in and you realise it's time to think about food for chilly weather. There are still leaves of spiky sorrel in the garden, and you don't need many for this soup – just enough to lift the creamy colour. For a touch of class, treat your guests to a caviar garnish. In the summer you can serve this soup lightly chilled.
SERVES 6

1 large cauliflower, stalks discarded,
   florets chopped
1 medium potato, peeled and chopped
½ onion, chopped
15g butter
1 tablespoon olive oil
1 litre Light chicken stock (page 184)
   or Vegetable nage (page 184)

500ml creamy milk
100ml double cream
6 large sorrel leaves, stalks trimmed
   and then shredded
2 tablespoons caviar (optional)
sea salt and freshly ground black pepper

1 Place the cauliflower florets, potato and onion in a saucepan with the butter and oil. Heat gently and, when the contents start to sizzle, cover with a lid and sweat everything over a low heat for about 10 minutes. The vegetables should not be at all coloured.
2 Add the stock or nage and bring to the boil, then pour in the milk and return gently to a boil. (This way, there will be no scum forming from the milk.) Season to taste, then simmer, uncovered, for 10–15 minutes when the vegetables should be soft.
3 Pour in half the cream, then purée in a food processor or blender, or whiz in the pan with a hand-held stick blender. Pass the purée through a sieve into a clean pan, rubbing with the back of a ladle.
4 Stir in the rest of the cream. Taste for seasoning and bring the soup to the boil. Ladle into soup plates, top with the sorrel shreds and add a spoonful of caviar to each. Serve straightaway.

Smoked haddock and mustard chowder

In Scotland they call a thick haddock and potato soup like this Cullen Skink, but I call this recipe a chowder so you all know what to expect. Do make sure you use natural undyed smoked haddock. My French training tempted me to add some coarsegrain French mustard, to celebrate the auld alliance. For a smart garnish, boil 4 quail's eggs for 2½ minutes, then peel and halve. Set on the soup just before serving. **SERVES 4**

1 large undyed Finnan haddock fillet, 400–500g
500ml milk
2 large waxy potatoes (such as Desirée),
   about 300g each
2 tablespoons olive oil
1 large shallot, chopped
100ml dry white wine
500ml Fish stock (page 184)
90ml double cream
1 heaped tablespoon coarsegrain mustard
sea salt and freshly ground black pepper

1 Cut the haddock fillet in two or three pieces to fit into a large saucepan. Bring the milk to the boil in the saucepan, then slip in the 'haddie' fillet. Remove the pan from the heat and leave for about 10 minutes. By then the fish will feel firm when pressed.
2 Lift out the fish, then strain the milk and reserve. Skin and flake the fish whilst still warm. Set aside.
3 Peel the potatoes and cut into small dice. Heat the oil and sauté the potatoes with the shallot for about 10 minutes, stirring occasionally, until lightly coloured. Add the wine and cook until reduced right down, then pour in the stock and reserved milk. Season and bring to the boil, stirring once or twice. Simmer for 15 minutes until the potatoes feel just tender.
4 Whiz the mixture until smooth, either in the pan with a hand-held stick blender or decanted into a food processor or blender.
5 Return to the pan, if necessary, and blend in the cream. Briskly stir in the mustard and check the seasoning again. Gradually stir in the flaked haddie, reheat gently and serve.

Thai chicken soup

Nearly everyone loves chicken soup because it is warming, wholesome and very tasty. I love the flavours of Thai cooking and enjoy experimenting with the ingredients that are becoming increasingly easier to buy. They work well in a chicken soup. You need a nice clear and bright stock for this soup, so follow my tips. **SERVES 4**

1 litre Light chicken stock (page 184)

2 stalks fresh lemon grass, chopped

1 red, 1 yellow and 1 green pepper,
   finely diced

1 plump fresh red chilli, seeded
   and finely chopped

3 tablespoons olive or groundnut oil

4 baby pak choi

2 skinless, boneless chicken breasts,
   about 100g each, diced small

¼ teaspoon mild curry powder

a generous pinch of cayenne pepper
   or chilli powder

2 tablespoons coconut cream

leaves from 1 sprig fresh basil (ideally
   Thai holy basil, but Italian is fine)

sea salt and freshly ground black pepper

1 Tie up the lemon grass in a muslin bag (or use a clean J-Cloth). In a large saucepan, lightly sauté the diced peppers, fresh chilli and lemon grass bag in half the oil for about 5 minutes, stirring occasionally. Add the pak choi and continue cooking for 2 minutes until wilted. Set aside.

2 Heat the remaining oil in a clean non-stick frying pan and stir-fry the diced chicken with the curry powder and cayenne or chilli powder until just firm and a lovely golden brown colour, about 5 minutes. Remove and cool on kitchen paper towel.

3 Add the chicken to the peppers and chilli. Stir in the coconut cream and stock. Bring to the boil and check the seasoning, then tear in the basil leaves. Pull out the bag of lemon grass at the last minute.

4 Serve hot in warmed bowls, making sure each diner has a pak choi.

Note Here are some helpful hints for making a clear stock. Before you begin, check that the chicken carcasses are well cleaned and free of any blood spots – it is best to rinse them under a cold tap. Simmer the stock rather than boil and, when cooked, allow it to stand for a good 15 minutes so the solids settle to the bottom of the pan. Then very gently pour through a muslin-lined sieve, leaving the solids and 'debris' behind.

Potage of potato and leek

This is just the sort of soup someone learning to cook should begin with. But although simple it can be turned into the ultimate in sophistication simply by adding a few lightly poached oysters or topping with small spoonfuls of whipped cream and Osietra caviar. **SERVES 4**

250g leeks (the white and pale
  green only), diced
1 small onion, chopped
1 tablespoon olive oil
15g butter
50ml dry white wine
1 large potato, about 300g,
  peeled and chopped

1 fresh bouquet garni (a few parsley
  stalks,
  sprig fresh thyme, small bay leaf and
  sprig of celery leaves tied together)
750ml Light chicken stock (page 184)
  or Vegetable nage (page 184)
100ml single cream
sea salt and freshly ground black pepper

1 Put the leeks and onion Into a large saucepan with the oil and butter. When they start to sizzle, cover and sweat the vegetables over a low heat for 5 minutes.

2 Add the wine and cook uncovered until evaporated. Add the potato and bouquet garni, cover with the stock or nage and bring to the boil. Season and simmer for 15 minutes until the potato is soft.

3 Remove the bouquet garni. You can leave this soup chunky, as the vegetables are chopped small, and the potato should by now have dissolved into the liquid, thickening it slightly. However, if you favour a silky texture, then purée either in a food processor or blender, or in the pan with a hand-held stick blender.

4 Stir in the cream and season to taste. A good soup for any meal occasion.

Starters and light dishes

Pillows of ricotta gnocchi with peas and fèves

If you have the impression that gnocchi is doughy and boring, then let me persuade you to try making potato gnocchi. They are much lighter than semolina gnocchi. Anyone who enjoys pottering about the kitchen and cooking should have a grand time with these!
SERVES 4

1kg large waxy potatoes
   (preferably Desirée or Maris Piper)
175g plain flour, plus extra for shaping
1 tablespoon fine sea salt
1 teaspoon freshly ground pepper
   (preferably white)
1 free-range egg, beaten

100g ricotta cheese
75g butter
200g podded fresh peas
200g podded fresh baby *fèves* (broad beans)
3 tablespoons Vinaigrette (page 184)
2 tablespoons chopped fresh parsley
sea salt and freshly ground black pepper

1 Boil the potatoes still in their skins until just tender. Drain and peel them whilst hot. (We do this wearing rubber gloves to protect our hands – fondly referred to by my young commis as 'the Marigolds'). Cut each potato into quarters and spread out on a baking sheet.

2 Dry off in the oven preheated to 200°C, Gas 6 for about 5 minutes. Then mash until smooth. The best way to do this is to push the potato through a ricer. Failing that a masher will do, but not an electric beater or food processor, or the texture will become gluey.

3 Mix the potato with the flour, fine sea salt, white pepper, egg and ricotta cheese. The mixture will be like a soft dough. Don't overbeat or the gnocchi will be tough. Spread out the mixture on a plate and chill until firm.

4 Shape the potato mixture into long cigar shapes about 1.5cm thick. Using the back of a table knife, cut across into 3cm lengths. Bring a large pan of water to the boil. Add the gnocchi pillows and simmer for about 5 minutes. (You may have to cook them in batches.) Drain well and plunge immediately into ice-cold water. Drain again and pat dry on kitchen paper towel.

5 Melt the butter and heat slowly until it turns a light brown colour. Strain though a fine sieve and discard the solids. Pour the butter into a frying pan and lightly fry the gnocchi until nicely coloured all over. Season and keep warm.

6 Meanwhile, cook the peas and *fèves* in lightly salted boiling water for 2–3 minutes. Drain and season. Stir in the vinaigrette to bind and then the parsley.

7 Divide the pea and *fève* salad among four plates and top with the browned gnocchi. Serve immediately.

Sweetcorn and spring onion risotto

The Italians serve risotto as a starter, whilst the French often use it as an accompaniment to a main course. I find it really versatile, as it can also make a light main dish. The basic recipe is always the same – it's the flavour variations that give character. This is a light, refreshing dish using the first of the summer sweetcorn. Always buy sweetcorn cobs still dressed in their green husks – those sold wrapped in plastic, which you find in many supermarkets, will have lost their 'just picked' fresh juiciness. Instead of enriching the tender rice grains with mascarpone, I stir in a purée of creamed sweetcorn. SERVES 4 AS A STARTER OR 3 AS A LIGHT MEAL

500–600ml Vegetable nage (page 184)
 or Light chicken stock (page 184)
1 large sweetcorn cob, still in its husk
1 shallot, finely chopped
3 tablespoons olive oil
200g risotto rice (Carnaroli, Arborio or Vialone Nano)
about 4 tablespoons dry white wine
2 spring onions, cut in thin rounds
200g can creamed sweetcorn
3 tablespoons freshly grated Parmesan cheese
a good knob of unsalted butter
sea salt and freshly ground black pepper

1 Put the nage or stock into a pan and heat to a gentle simmer.
2 Pull the green husks and the silky yellow threads from the corn cob. Stand the cob upright, tapered end down. Using a sharp heavy-bladed cook's knife, cut straight down the cob, releasing the small square kernels. Discard the central core, and scoop the kernels into a bowl. (They might have popped out all over the worktop.)
3 In a large saucepan, gently sauté the shallot in 2 tablespoons of the oil for about 5 minutes until softened but not coloured. Stir in the remaining tablespoon of oil and the sweetcorn kernels. Cook for a minute or so, then add the rice and cook for a minute, stirring.
4 Pour in the wine and cook until it has reduced away, then ladle in a quarter of the nage or stock. Bring to the boil, stirring, then turn down to a medium heat and continue bubbling gently until the liquid has been absorbed. Spoon in another ladleful of nage or stock and repeat the process, still stirring. Continue adding liquid in ladlefuls, waiting for each batch to be absorbed and stirring often, until the rice is plump and just tender but not soft. This should take about 15 minutes. (You may not need all the nage or stock.)
5 Stir in the spring onions and cook for a minute or two to heat. Then gradually stir in the creamed corn, half the Parmesan and the butter. When hot, season well and serve immediately in shallow bowls, topped with more Parmesan.

Pumpkin and pancetta risotto

It is a poor autumn kitchen indeed that does not have a plump pumpkin available. There are so many ways to take advantage of its creamy, sweet golden flesh, from soups and stews through to pasta fillings and dessert pies. A risotto with a lightly browned diced pumpkin brunoise, some smoky crisp pancetta and tangy Parmesan makes a good light meal. SERVES 4 AS A STARTER OR 3 AS A LIGHT MEAL

40g pancetta, chopped
500–600ml Light chicken stock (page 184)
2 large shallots, chopped
500g pumpkin flesh, cut into 1cm cubes
3 tablespoons olive oil
200g risotto rice (Carnaroli, Arborio or Vialone Nano)
100ml dry white wine
2 tablespoons mascarpone
25g freshly grated Parmesan cheese
sea salt and freshly ground black pepper

1 Heat a dry non-stick frying pan and, when hot, fry the pancetta until browned and crisp. Drain and set aside. Heat the stock to a gentle simmer in a saucepan.
2 In a large saucepan, gently sauté the shallots and pumpkin in the oil for about 5 minutes. Stir in the rice and cook for another 2 minutes to toast the grains. Pour in the wine and cook until reduced right down.
3 Now pour in a quarter of the stock and stir well. Cook gently until the liquid has been absorbed, then stir in another ladleful of stock. Continue cooking and stirring, gradually adding the stock, until the rice grains are just tender. The whole process should take about 15 minutes.
4 About 2 minutes before the end of cooking, stir in the pancetta, mascarpone and half of the Parmesan. Check the seasoning, then serve in warmed bowls, sprinkled with the remaining Parmesan.

Warm salad of ceps and white asparagus

White asparagus is popular in Europe, where it is associated with fine dining. The spears are almost always served whole. Between April and May I am able to buy plump white asparagus grown in the Vale of Evesham. It is so tender there is no need for any peeling, just a thin trimming of the stalk end. It makes a good simple salad, topped with sautéed sliced ceps and a brown butter sauce. **SERVES 4**

about 12 large spears, or 24–30 thinner
  spears, fresh white asparagus
juice of 1 lemon
4 tablespoons olive oil
75g unsalted butter
200g fresh ceps, bases trimmed, sliced
2 tablespoons fresh flat-leaf parsley leaves
sea salt and freshly ground black pepper

1 Prepare the asparagus first. Trim the ends. Bring a shallow pan of salted water to the boil and add half of the lemon juice and a tablespoon of the oil. Add the asparagus spears and blanch for about 4 minutes, then drain carefully (so as not to damage the tips) and plunge into a wide shallow bowl of iced water. Leave until cold, then drain carefully again and pat lightly dry.

2 Make the brown butter. Heat the butter gently in a small saucepan, then turn up the heat and cook until the butter just turns brown. Watch it like a hawk! Tip it quickly into a cup to stop the browning. Set aside.

3 Heat the remaining oil in a frying pan and fry the ceps, stirring and tossing, until just softened. Add the parsley leaves, season and remove to a plate.

4 Wipe out the pan and tip in the brown butter, leaving the solids behind in the cup. Heat gently, then lay in the asparagus spears. Heat carefully until hot, then sprinkle over the rest of the lemon juice.

5 Arrange 4 asparagus spears on each plate, drizzle over any pan juices and spoon over the ceps. That's it – naturally simple.

Tomato and Parmesan gratinée tarts

Autumn sees the abundance of plump, full-flavoured plum tomatoes, which I enjoy serving pizza-style on discs of light crisp pastry. The tomato slices are bound with melted Parmesan shavings and then placed on top of the pastry just before serving. A bouquet of rocket salad tops each tart. SERVES 4

300g Puff pastry, preferably home-made (page 185)
8 large, ripe plum tomatoes, skinned
2 tablespoons balsamic vinegar
2 tablespoons olive oil
1 tablespoon chopped fresh chervil
1 tablespoon chopped fresh parsley
50g fresh Parmesan, shaved with a swivel peeler
100g wild rocket
1–2 tablespoons Vinaigrette (page 184)
sea salt and freshly ground black pepper

1 Roll out the pastry to a thickness of a £1 coin. Cut out four rounds about 12cm diameter, using a saucer or small plate as a guide. Place on a heavy baking sheet and chill for 20 minutes.
2 Preheat the oven to 200°C, Gas 6. Bake the pastry for 10 minutes, then place another baking sheet on top to press the rounds down and keep them flat. Bake for a further 8–10 minutes until just golden. Remove to a wire rack to cool and crisp.
3 Slice the tomatoes evenly and arrange on another baking sheet in four overlapping circles about the same size as the pastry rounds (certainly no larger). Brush with the balsamic vinegar and oil, season and sprinkle with the herbs. Lay the Parmesan shavings on top, making sure they connect with all the tomato slices – as they melt, the shavings will hold the tomato together.
4 Preheat the grill to the highest setting. When really hot, place the tomatoes under the grill near to the heat. The cheese should start to melt almost immediately. Watch carefully – the cheese doesn't need to brown, just melt so it holds the tomato slices together.
5 Remove from the grill and wait a few seconds, then using a fish slice transfer each round of tomato on to a pastry round.
6 Season the rocket and toss with the vinaigrette. Pile on top of each tart and serve immediately.

Salade tiède of mousserons, mussels and crosnes

This is a good example of a style of dish the French call 'terre et mer' – mixing foods of land and sea. It is a warm salad of mussels and two unusual ingredients found only during the autumn, mousserons and crosnes. Mousserons are tiny, perfectly formed mushrooms with caps the size of Smarties. Their fairy size gives a false impression, for they are tough little things and respond well to high frying. Crosnes, or Chinese artichokes, are 'wild' artichokes with a good earthy flavour. They both need particular preparation. **SERVES 4**

100g mousseron mushrooms
25g butter
2 tablespoons olive oil
300g fresh mussels
1 bay leaf
1 sprig fresh thyme
100ml dry white wine
100g crosnes (or use baby Jerusalem artichokes)
1 tablespoon chopped fresh chervil or parsley
2 tablespoons double cream
sea salt and freshly ground black pepper

1 Prepare this dish in stages, then bring everything together just before serving. First, the mousserons. Pick off the stalks so you just have the caps. Heat half the butter in a frying pan and sauté them for 2–3 minutes until softened.

2 Drain off the juice and save it in a small saucepan. Wipe out the frying pan, then heat the remaining butter with a teaspoon of the oil until nice and hot. Sauté the mousserons again to get them nice and browned. Drain, saving the juices again, and set aside.

3 Wash the mussels well and pull off any beards. Scrub off the barnacles too, if possible. Discard any mussels that don't close when you tap them. Heat an empty saucepan until very hot and tip in the mussels, together with the bay leaf, thyme and wine. Clamp on the lid and cook for about 4 minutes.

4 Uncover the pan and drain the liquid into the saucepan with the mousseron juices. Discard any mussels that haven't opened. Pick out the meat of those that have and cool, then chill for 30 minutes to firm the flesh.

5 To prepare the crosnes, top and tail if necessary, then place in a bowl with a little cold water and rub them between your hands with sea salt. This helps to scrub them clean. Rinse well.

6 Heat the remaining oil in a pan and sauté the crosnes until nicely coloured, about 3 minutes. Tip the mussels into the pan and stir-fry until reheated. Toss in the mousserons and reheat, then divide among four soup plates. Sprinkle with the chervil or parsley.

7 Add the cream to the saved juices and bubble down until reduced by half. Nappé the salad – there will be just enough sauce to moisten everything – and serve.

A special salade niçoise

Fresh tuna is a must for this ultimate summer salad. I suggest you look for line-caught blue fin tuna, although yellow fin makes fine eating too. Ask for a loin cut, and avoid any fish with bruised flesh or blood lines. The recipe is quite straightforward, but I like to add a touch of luxury and use little quail's eggs instead of the usual quartered hen's ones. **SERVES 4**

12 quail's eggs

3 tablespoons white wine vinegar

100g thin French beans, topped
  and tailed, then halved if liked

150g baby new potatoes

100ml Vinaigrette (page 184)
  mixed with 3 tablespoons double cream

4 firm plum tomatoes, skinned

50g salted anchovies (the ones sold loose)

50g fresh black olives

200g mixed baby salad leaves
  (such as the tips of frisée or oak leaf
  lettuce, wild rocket, baby Cos)

4 tuna loin steaks, about 100g each

1–2 tablespoons olive oil

1 tablespoon balsamic vinegar

sea salt and freshly ground black pepper

1 There are lots of stages for this recipe, so get everything prepared first. The cooked quail's eggs will be easier to peel if first soaked in cold water to cover, mixed with the 3 tablespoons vinegar, for 20 minutes. This breaks down the tough albumen in the shells. Then drain and cook for 2 minutes in boiling water. Drain and plunge into a bowl of cold water to cool for 10 minutes. Peel and leave whole.

2 Blanch the green beans in boiling water for 2 minutes, drain and refresh in ice-cold water. Drain again.

3 Cook the baby new potatoes for 12 minutes until just tender. Drain and toss in 2 tablespoons of the cream dressing. Leave to cool.

4 Quarter each tomato lengthways and scoop out the seeds. Leave them as petal shapes or slice in half again.

5 Rinse the anchovies in tepid water, then cut into a rough dice. Stone and slice the olives.

6 Pick over the salad leaves. Mix with the green beans and toss with the remaining dressing. Divide the leaves and beans among four large shallow bowls or dinner plates. Scatter over the anchovies, tomatoes and olives. Arrange the potatoes and eggs around the leaves.

7 Now cook the tuna steaks. Heat a large, heavy non-stick frying pan until you can feel a good heat rising. Add a little oil, then lay in the tuna steaks. Cook for 1–2 minutes on each side until they feel lightly springy when pressed. The tuna should still be pink in the centre. If you like yours more cooked, then allow longer, but don't cook too well done or the flesh will be dry and chewy. Deglaze with the balsamic vinegar. Season and lift out of the pan.

8 Cut each steak in half and lay on top of the waiting salads. Serve straightaway.

Salad of ceps and langoustines in mustard dressing

Langoustines (aka Dublin Bay prawns) are sold in three sizes, from 1 to 3. I generally opt for the biggest, size 1, because the flesh is plump and sweet and remains moist when pan-roasted. To make them easier to peel, blanch just for 1 minute in boiling water. Apart from this, the salad is straightforward to prepare, and the colours and flavours come together well on the plate.
SERVES 4

12 large langoustines
3 tablespoons olive oil
200g large fresh ceps, bases trimmed,
  then thickly sliced
150ml Vinaigrette (page 184)
1 slightly rounded tablespoon Dijon mustard
150g baby spinach leaves
a few good pinches of mild curry powder
sea salt and freshly ground black pepper
celery leaves, deep fried if you like, to garnish

1 Bring a large pan of salted water to the boil, then drop in the langoustines. Boil for a minute, then drain and cool. When you are able to handle them (they are easier to peel when warm), pull off the heads and crack the top of the shell with the back of a knife. Then simply push up from the tail end and out should pop perfectly peeled, pink shellfish. Set aside.

2 Heat 2 tablespoons of the oil in a frying pan and, when really hot, sauté the ceps until they are nicely coloured and softened. Season well. Remove and cool.

3 Mix the vinaigrette with the mustard. Toss the ceps with a third of the dressing. Set aside. Season the spinach and toss with another third of the dressing. Place in the centre of four plates. (In the restaurant we arrange the spinach leaves in a flower shape inside a large plain cutter – not possible, I know, when you are on your own.)

4 Season the langoustines and dust with pinches of curry power. Heat the last of the oil in a frying pan and, when really hot, sauté the langoustines quickly for a minute or two on each side. Cut each one in half, if large.

5 Spoon the mustardy ceps in the centre of the spinach, then top with the langoustines. Finally, trickle over the last of the dressing, garnish with celery leaves and serve quickly.

Scottish lobster with mango and spinach salad

This dish is a real treat for the eye – simply stunning colours of pink, gold and deep green. I would advise that for the best flavour you cook your own lobsters (put them in the freezer first to make them sleepy). Another useful hint is that it is easier to shell lobsters whilst they are still warm. **SERVES 4**

Court bouillon (page 184)
4 small live lobsters, about 700g each
2 just ripe mangoes
3 tablespoons Vinaigrette (page 184)
150g baby spinach leaves
sea salt and freshly ground black pepper

1 Bring the court bouillon to a gentle boil in a large pan, then drop in the lobsters. Poach them gently for 5–6 minutes. Remove the pan from the heat and allow the lobsters to cool a little in the bouillon.

2 When the lobsters are cool enough for you to handle (wear rubber gloves), remove them and take the meat from the shells. Use strong kitchen scissors or poultry shears to cut through the body shell, and take out the meat in one piece. Check the third disc along for the dirt sac and pull this out. Extract the meat from the claws and knuckles by cracking the shells with the back of the knife. Chop the claw and knuckle meat. Pop all the shelled meat back into the bouillon and leave to cool down. When cold, remove and drain.

3 Peel the mangoes, cut the flesh off the central stone and chop into small dice. Toss with half the vinaigrette.

4 Toss the spinach leaves in the remaining vinaigrette and season well. Arrange the spinach in the centre of four plates (we arrange ours in a petal pattern).

5 Scatter over the dressed mango. Put the lobster knuckle and claw meat in the centre. Slice the lobster tail meat into medallions and arrange on top of the mango, then serve.

Salad of avocado and crab with pink grapefruit dressing

You cannot beat classic combinations of flavour and colour – avocado and seafood win fans every time. But instead of a creamy mayonnaise-style dressing, try mixing the seafood – here crab – with a light vinaigrette spiked with star-burst bubbles of pink grapefruit. The pastel shades and fresh flavours will make this a very popular starter.

Fresh crab meat is the best choice. If you have to use frozen, press the crab meat in a colander using the back of a ladle, to remove all excess liquid. **SERVES 4**

1 pink grapefruit
150ml Vinaigrette (page 184)
2 large, just ripe avocados
2 plum tomatoes, skinned, seeded and chopped
juice of ½ lime
1 teaspoon finely chopped shallot or spring onion
few drops of hot pepper sauce (optional)
150g white crab meat
about 100g small salad leaves (a mixture, or
   mâche or small wild rocket leaves alone)
sea salt and freshly ground black pepper

1 Cut the peel and pith from the grapefruit, then using a sharp fruit knife cut between the membranes to release the segments. (Do this over a bowl to catch the juice.) Add the segments to the bowl and break into tiny 'teardrops' with the tines of a fork. Mix in 100ml of the vinaigrette and set aside.

2 Make a guacamole. Halve and stone the avocados and scoop out the flesh into a shallow bowl. Mash to a chunky purée using a fork, then mix in the tomatoes, lime juice, shallot or onion, pepper sauce to taste (if using) and seasoning.

3 Carefully check the crab meat for any bits of shell. (We do this on a flat plate with the back of a fork.) Season nicely and bind with 1 tablespoon of the remaining vinaigrette.

4 Toss the salad leaves with the last of the vinaigrette, and season too.

5 To assemble the salad, use a large plain scone cutter 7–8cm in diameter. Place the cutter in the centre of a medium plate and spoon in a quarter of the guacamole. Lightly press a quarter of the crab meat on top, then make little towering piles of salad leaves on top of that. Gently lift off the cutter. Wipe the cutter inside, and repeat three more times on three more plates. (Alternatively, you can simply spoon the three salads on top of each other on the plates.)

6 Finally, dribble tiny teaspoonfuls of the grapefruit dressing around each salad and serve.

Steamed scallops and asparagus with lemon grass butter sauce

Whoever said steamed food was boring? Not me. For example, I love the pure delicate flavours of sweet scallops and pencil-thin asparagus steamed in their own juices, then gently coated in a fragrant beurre blanc. Ask the fishmonger to open the scallops for you, and to give you the cup-shaped shells. In the restaurant we usually throw away the corals, but you can cook them if you wish. Chinese bamboo steaming baskets are cheap and easy to find if you take a trip to any major Chinatown. I use them often for fish and vegetables. SERVES 4

4–6 large scallops, removed from their shells, with 4 of the rounded shells saved
150g thin green asparagus tips
1 tablespoon chopped fresh chervil or chives
sea salt and freshly ground black pepper

Sauce
1 stalk fresh lemon grass, tough outer leaves stripped off
2 shallots, finely chopped
100ml dry white wine
1 teaspoon white wine vinegar
2 tablespoons double cream
100g unsalted butter, chilled and cut in small cubes

1 Rinse the scallops well and pat dry. Feel for the hard nugget of flesh on the side and pull this off. Very plump scallops are best sliced horizontally in three, otherwise simply slice in half.
2 Scrub out the shells and divide the asparagus among them. Season lightly and place the scallop slices on top, adding the corals if you are using them.
3 Prepare a pan of boiling water over which your bamboo steamer will rest. While the water is heating, make the butter sauce.
4 Chop the lemon grass very finely, discarding any hard woody bits. Wrap and tie up in a piece of muslin. Cook the shallots and lemon grass in the white wine for about 5 minutes until nicely softened and the liquid has reduced right down to almost nothing. Remove the lemon grass bag. Add the vinegar and cook until evaporated, which takes seconds.
5 Stir in the cream, season and bring to a simmer. (The cream helps to stabilise the sauce.) Drop in a couple of cubes of butter and beat vigorously with a small whisk until melted and emulsified. Drop in some more butter cubes and whisk again. When all the cubes have been added, mix in 2 tablespoons of cold water and remove from the heat. Cover the top of the sauce with cling film or a butter paper and set aside to keep warm.
6 Bring the pan of water to a good head of steam. Season the scallops and place the shells in the basket base. Place over the pan and cover with the lid. Steam for 3½–4 minutes, depending on how thick the scallops are.
7 Remove the basket from the pan – take care as steam can burn badly. Lift out the shells carefully so as not to spill any juice, and put on plates, setting each shell on a small mound of rock salt. (The salt helps to keep the shells level so they don't tip over.)
8 Nappé the scallops with the butter sauce, sprinkle with the herbs and serve right away.

Fricassée of scallops and girolles with lettuce sauce

Girolles, the little, golden fairy-like mushrooms with a divine flavour, are one of the culinary delights of summer. They need to be peeled at the stalk end, but after that is done this is quite a quick dish to put together. (Out of season, you may like to use dried girolles, which can be restored by soaking and then patting dry.) Make sure the scallops you use are plump king scallops – mine are hand-dived in cold Scottish waters. The sauce is unusual, a light cream of lettuce. In the restaurant we also garnish this with whole garlic cloves confit in goose fat until the skins become crispy. An ideal dish served as a light summery lunch. SERVES 4

300g small summer girolles
1 large Little Gem or small Cos
   lettuce, shredded
1 clove garlic, peeled and left whole
50g smoked lean bacon, chopped
4 spring onions, chopped
4–6 tablespoons olive oil
100ml Vinaigrette (page 184)
juice of ½ small lemon

1 tablespoon chopped fresh chives,
   plus extra for sprinkling
1 tablespoon chopped fresh chervil,
   plus extra sprigs to garnish
6 large fresh scallops, removed
   from their shells, without corals
½ teaspoon mild curry powder
sea salt and freshly ground black pepper

1 Using a small sharp knife, trim the ends of the girolles. Set aside.

2 Make the sauce. Sauté the lettuce with the garlic clove, bacon and one of the spring onions in 1 tablespoon of the oil until wilted, 3–5 minutes. Remove the garlic clove and discard. Whiz the lettuce, bacon and onion plus any pan juices in a food processor, then pass through a sieve into another small pan, rubbing with the back of a ladle. Season, return the sauce to a simmer and cook for 3 minutes to reduce down by about a third. Beat in the vinaigrette and set aside.

3 Heat a frying pan with 2 tablespoons of the oil and sauté the girolles and the rest of the spring onions with the lemon juice, stirring occasionally, for about 3 minutes. Season and mix in the chopped herbs. Set aside and keep warm.

4 When you are ready to serve, heat the last of the oil in a frying pan. Add the scallops, arranging them in a circle. Season nicely and sprinkle over the curry powder. After 2 minutes, turn the scallops, in the same order you placed them in the pan, and cook the other side until nicely golden, 1–2 minutes. Season again. The scallops should feel quite bouncy when pressed lightly. Don't overcook them. Slice each in half horizontally.

5 To serve, spoon the girolle mixture in the centre of four warmed plates and arrange the scallops on top. Spoon the sauce around and finish with a sprinkling of chives and a sprig of chervil.

Seafood in a nage
with carrot spaghetti

This is my version of a plat de fruits de mer – a glorious collection of favourite seafood served in a light aromatic vegetable broth scented with star anise. It is served with a thin 'spaghetti' of carrots, which can be cut on a razor-sharp mandolin or food processor attachment. **SERVES 4**

2 carrots
70g butter
500ml Vegetable nage (page 184)
3 star anise
150g baby clams in shells
3 tablespoons dry white wine
8 rock oysters
4 large scallops, removed from
　their shells, without corals
2 tablespoons double cream
a good squeeze of lemon juice
1 heaped tablespoon shredded fresh basil
sea salt and freshly ground black pepper

1 First, cut the carrots into long thin 'spaghetti' using a mandolin, Japanese slicer or an equivalent slicer blade on a food processor. Bring the butter and 3 tablespoons of nage to the boil. Stir in the carrot spaghetti, season and cover. Cook for 1 minute, then set aside.
2 Heat the rest of the nage until boiling. Add the star anise, then remove from the heat and infuse for 10 minutes. Discard the anise.
3 Heat a large saucepan and, when hot, add the clams and wine. Clamp on the lid and cook for 3–5 minutes, shaking the pan occasionally, until the shells open. Discard any clams whose shells remain steadfastly shut. Pick the meat from the shells and set aside. Strain and save the juice.
4 Open the oysters, saving the juice (if the fishmonger does this, be sure to ask him to save the juice). Cut each scallop horizontally in three.
5 Reheat the nage and slip in the slices of scallops. Heat on a bare simmer, then add the oysters and cook for 1 minute. Finally, drop in the shelled clams. Stir in the saved juices too. Check the seasoning, and stir in the cream, lemon juice and basil.
6 As soon as everything is hot, divide the seafood among four soup bowls and ladle over the hot stock. Top with the carrot spaghetti and serve.

Marinated tuna salad

Tuna is a dense, meaty fish so you need a smaller portion size than other fish, no more than 100g. The flesh is also affected by the way it is caught – the tail end is less likely to have any signs of congealed blood. So try to buy a piece of loin from the tail end. After searing in hot oil, marinate the tuna in a coriander-flavoured dressing. Then serve with soused autumnal vegetables. SERVES 4–6

400g loin of tuna, from the tail end

3 tablespoons olive oil

150ml Vinaigrette (page 184)

1 teaspoon coriander berries, lightly crushed

1 tablespoon chopped fresh coriander

2 sticks salsify

a good squeeze of lemon juice

2 globe artichokes

100g mangetout, chopped

1 small onion, sliced

2 medium carrots, thinly sliced

2 tablespoons aged balsamic vinegar

sea salt and freshly ground black pepper

1 Slice the tuna loin into two long fillets. Heat 1 tablespoon of the oil in a heavy-based frying pan (or a ridged griddle pan if you want attractive chargrilled stripes on the tuna). Sear the fillets for 2 minutes all over – the flesh should still feel a little springy. Do not overcook tuna, as it will toughen and dry out. Transfer to a dish.

2 Mix half the vinaigrette with the coriander berries, then pour over the tuna fillets. Press the fresh coriander over the surface. Cover and leave to steep for 1 hour.

3 Meanwhile, peel the salsify and cut into sticks. Cook in boiling salted water with the lemon juice for 5 minutes. Remove with a slotted spoon, refresh and set aside.

4 Cut off the artichoke stalks, pull off the leaves and cut out the hairy choke to leave the meaty heart. Cut the heart into pieces. Cook in the lemon water for 10 minutes. Drain.

5 Blanch the mangetout in boiling water for 1 minute, then drain and refresh under cold running water. Drain and pat dry.

6 Heat the remaining oil in a saucepan, add the onion and cook for 3 minutes. Add the carrots, salsify and artichokes, and cook for a further 2–3 minutes. Finally, toss in the blanched mangetout and cook for 1 minute. Season nicely and stir in the balsamic vinegar and then the rest of the vinaigrette. Set aside to cool.

7 To serve, remove the tuna from the marinade (no need to scrape off the herbs unless you wish to). Cut the fillets into medallions. Divide the soused vegetables among the plates and place the tuna medallions on top of them.

Salad of queen scallops, baby calamari and confit new potatoes

Dainty, pretty and in a class of its own, this is an elegant starter for a special summer dinner. You need the very small baby calamari, sold ready cleaned with the tentacles pushed inside the bodies. The small queen scallops, which look quite enchanting in their little shells, are becoming more available in quality fishmongers. They are sometimes sold in nets, although some shops sell them ready shelled. If so, check they are not frozen, or the flesh will taste watery. For the potatoes, use little Jersey Royals, in their brief season, or try baby Ratte or Anya varieties. Incidentally, you can now buy goose fat in cans. Even my local supermarket sells it.
SERVES 4

200g baby new potatoes
  (the smaller the better)
100g goose fat
200ml tepid milk
120g plain flour
1 teaspoon easy-blend dried yeast
4 baby calamari, about 75g each
about 32–40 queen scallops,
  removed from their shells

a few good pinches of mild curry powder
some light olive oil, for frying
4–6 tablespoons Vinaigrette (page 184)
  mixed with 2 teaspoons chopped fresh tarragon
about 300g mixed salad leaves (varieties with
  soft leaves such as mâche or oak leaf)
sea salt and freshly ground black pepper

1 First, confit the potatoes, which has to be done on a very low heat. You may find a metal heat diffuser useful. Put the potatoes and goose fat into a small saucepan – the potatoes should be covered in the fat. Cook on the lowest heat setting for 20–25 minutes until just tender. The fat may bubble occasionally, but don't let it get any hotter. The potatoes should cook, not fry. Drain on kitchen paper towel and cool. Save the fat.

2 Whiz the milk, flour, yeast and a good pinch of salt to a thick batter in a food processor or blender. Tip into a shallow bowl and set aside in the fridge for 1 hour.

3 Check the calamari are clean inside, then pat dry.

4 Season the scallops with a little salt, pepper and curry powder to coat. Heat 1 tablespoon of oil in a frying pan and, when hot, add the scallops and quickly toss for less than a minute. Remove and drain, then toss in half the vinaigrette. Set aside.

5 Halve the new potatoes. Heat a tablespoon of the saved goose fat in a frying pan. When hot, quickly brown the potatoes until crispy, then drain and season. Keep warm.

6 Pick over the salad leaves, season and toss with the remaining vinaigrette. Mound in the centre of four large plates.

7 Heat about 1cm of oil in a frying pan. Remove the batter from the fridge and dip in the calamari bodies and tentacles, coating evenly. Lay them in the hot oil and cook for a couple of minutes on each side until crispy and golden. Do not overcook. Drain and season.

8 Spoon the scallops on top of the salad and sit the calamari on top of that. Arrange the potatoes around the salad and serve.

Wild duck salad
with hazelnut dressing

At the start of the game season you can buy small wild ducks with green necks (colverts), which are the size of a poussin. The flesh is much darker and more gamey than farmed duck. Although the legs are tough (it's all that summer swimming), the breasts make fine eating, especially in a warm salad with apple and celeriac. There are a number of stages to this recipe, but they are all simple and come together quickly at the end. SERVES 4

1 tablespoon olive oil

2 wild ducks, about 700g each

50g hazelnuts in skins

25g sultanas

200g celeriac

1 large, new season's Cox's apple

sea salt and freshly ground black pepper

Dressing

3 tablespoons groundnut oil

3 tablespoons hazelnut oil

1 tablespoon white wine vinegar

2 teaspoons sherry vinegar

a squeeze of lemon juice

1 Preheat the oven to 200°C, Gas 6. At the same time, heat the oil in a non-stick frying pan and brown the breasts of the birds, pressing the skin well on to the hot pan. Transfer the birds to a small roasting tin.

2 Roast the birds for 10–12 minutes, when the breasts should feel still slightly springy. You only need the breast meat so do not fret about the legs. Remove and set aside to rest for 15 minutes.

3 Meanwhile, roast the hazelnuts in the oven for about 10 minutes, watching them like a hawk so they do not burn, then rub them in a tea towel so the skins slip off. Chop the nuts. Soak the sultanas in boiling water to cover for 5 minutes so they plump up, then drain well.

4 Make the dressing by putting all the ingredients in a small jam jar, covering and shaking well to blend.

5 Peel the celeriac and cut into thin julienne strips. Mix with half the dressing, the sultanas and hazelnuts. Quarter, core and evenly chop the apple, leaving on the lovely blushed red and green skin. Mix with the celeriac salad.

6 Now, using a small, sharp filleting knife, slice off each duck breast in one piece. Carve each breast as thinly as you can. The flesh should be pink and lightly cooked. Lay the slices in a dish and season. Mix any of the duck juices that seep out with the rest of the dressing and drizzle over the duck breasts.

7 Lay the breast slices on top of the apple and celeriac salad, and serve as soon as possible.

Warm salad of pigeon with honey-soused vegetables

Here is another starter that makes good use of the best foods in season. Root vegetables make delicious salads if cooked briefly, then left to cool in a well-flavoured marinade. Game breasts cooked pink and sliced thinly complement them nicely. **SERVES 4**

100g celeriac
100g kohlrabi
1 small bulb fennel
100g baby onions
2–3 tablespoons olive oil
100g baby carrots, scraped
50g tiny mushrooms, such as girolles
   or mousserons, trimmed
15g butter
8 boneless wood pigeon breasts,
   about 75g each
sea salt and freshly ground black pepper

Marinade
1 shallot, finely chopped
1 tablespoon olive oil
1 sprig fresh thyme (lemon thyme if possible)
1 tablespoon sherry vinegar
1 tablespoon flower honey
100ml groundnut oil
50ml hazelnut oil
juice of 1 lime

1 First, make the marinade. Gently sauté the shallot in the olive oil with the thyme for about 5 minutes until softened but not coloured. Deglaze with the sherry vinegar and cook for a few seconds. Add the honey, groundnut and hazelnut oils, and the lime juice plus some seasoning. Keep warm.

2 Peel the celeriac and kohlrabi and cut into cubes or bâtons, varying the lengths and shapes to add interest. Keep the thicknesses even so the vegetables cook nicely. Peel the outside ribs of the fennel with a swivel peeler, then cut lengthways into wedges. Blanch the onions in boiling water for 2 minutes, then drain and peel.

3 Heat 1–2 tablespoons of olive oil in a heavy-based frying pan and stir in all the vegetables. Cook gently for 5–7 minutes, stirring occasionally, until they just begin to soften but without colouring them. Remove from the heat and pour over three-quarters of the marinade. Leave the vegetables to cool in this for at least 2 hours. Do not chill, as they should be at room temperature.

4 Now for the pigeon. Heat another tablespoon of olive oil with the butter in a heavy-based frying pan. Season the breasts and cook, skin side down, for about 3 minutes. Flip the breasts over and cook the other side for 2–3 minutes. They should feel lightly springy when pressed. Season again. Leave to rest for 3 minutes or so whilst you plate the vegetables.

5 Drain the vegetables of their marinade (this can be re-used should you wish). Divide among four plates. Slice the pigeon breasts on the diagonal, or leave them whole, and sit on top of the vegetables. Trickle over some of the remaining marinade and serve hot.

Summery quails in a tomato tarragon dressing

Quails look so inviting with their small plump breasts. Many people find them fiddly to eat, so we remove the breasts after roasting and cool them in a light tomato dressing. They are served on a warm salad of celery and summer girolles. A terrific starter. **SERVES 4**

4 fresh quails

6 tablespoons olive oil

½ small tomato, seeded
  and very finely chopped

½ shallot, very finely chopped

½ teaspoon tomato ketchup

½ teaspoon coarsegrain mustard

½ teaspoon fresh lemon juice

1 teaspoon chopped fresh tarragon

4 small sticks celery, cut into small
  lengths

100ml Chicken stock (page 184)
  or Vegetable nage (page 184)

70g fresh girolles, ends trimmed,
  then halved if large

a few celery leaves, to garnish
  (can be deep-fried, if liked)

sea salt and freshly ground black pepper

1 Preheat the oven to 190°C, Gas 5. Brush the quails lightly with a little of the oil, season and roast for 12 minutes.

2 Meanwhile, make a dressing by mixing together the finely chopped tomato, shallot, ketchup, mustard, lemon juice, tarragon and 3 tablespoons of the oil. Season well.

3 Remove the quails from the oven and allow to stand for 10 minutes. Using a sharp boning knife, remove the lightly cooked breasts, keeping them whole. (Use the carcasses in a stock.) Mix the breasts into the tomato dressing and set aside to cool.

4 Heat 1 tablespoon of the remaining oil in a small frying pan and sauté the celery until golden brown. Pour in the stock or nage, season nicely and cover the celery with a butter paper. Simmer for about 10 minutes until softened and the liquid has evaporated away.

5 Meanwhile, sauté the girolles in the last of the oil for about 5 minutes, stirring once or twice, then season.

6 To serve, place the celery in the centre of four dinner plates. Spoon the girolles on top. Arrange the quail breasts on top of that and trickle around any leftover dressing. Garnish with celery leaves.

Main courses

Sea trout with crushed fresh peas

Wild sea trout, like salmon, can live in fresh or salt water. Slightly sweeter than salmon and a little smaller, they are at their best between April and September. Superb fish needs just the simplest of accompaniments – in this case a crushed purée of fresh summer peas bound with a little vinaigrette and enhanced with some fresh marjoram. Serve with baby new potatoes.

SERVES 4

1 sea trout, about 2–2.5kg,
  filleted in two, skin on
1–2 tablespoons olive oil
500g fresh peas in pods, podded
1 tablespoon chopped fresh marjoram,
  plus marjoram leaves to garnish
2 tablespoons Vinaigrette (page 184)
sea salt and freshly ground black pepper

1 Feel the fish flesh for any pinbones with your fingertips and remove them with your fingernails or tweezers. Cut each fillet across in half. Trim these 4 pieces neatly. Using the tip of a very sharp knife (or a clean craft knife), score the skin in thin parallel lines, leaving a 1cm border uncut all round. Rub both sides of the fish with the oil and set aside.

2 Cook the peas in boiling salted water for 3–4 minutes until just tender. Drain and return to the pan. Crush the peas against the side of the pan with a fork so you have a chunky purée. Season, and stir in the chopped marjoram and vinaigrette. Set aside.

3 Heat a non-stick frying pan. When you can feel a good heat rising, place the fillets in the pan, skin side down. Season and cook for about 4 minutes so the skin becomes crispy. Carefully turn and cook the other side for a minute just to brown lightly. Season again.

4 Spoon the crushed peas into the centre of four warmed dinner plates and place the fish on top. Garnish with marjoram leaves, if liked, and serve.

Wild salmon with wilted lettuce and cucumber salad and a vine tomato butter sauce

The wild salmon season starts in February and lasts through the summer months. These free, wild cousins of farmed salmon have a darker, less fatty flesh and a fuller flavour. Out of season, the next best salmon is that reared in Scottish lochs, on a near natural (organic) diet, with artificial currents to encourage them to develop muscle. The salad and sauce here are both Mediterranean-inspired. **SERVES** 4

4 thick-cut fillets of wild salmon,
 about 150g each, skinned
3 tablespoons olive oil
1 large cucumber, peeled and diced
2 tomatoes, skinned, seeded and chopped
100g black olives, stoned and chopped
1 tablespoon chopped fresh parsley
2 baby Little Gem lettuces
3 tablespoons Vinaigrette (page 184)
sea salt and freshly ground black pepper

Sauce
250g vine-ripened tomatoes
1 teaspoon sherry vinegar
1 teaspoon caster sugar
1 tablespoon chopped fresh basil
100ml double cream
50g butter, diced

1 Rub both sides of the fillets with 1 tablespoon of the olive oil and set aside.

2 Mix together the cucumber, tomatoes, olives and parsley. Season well and set this salad aside.

3 Make the sauce: halve the tomatoes and whiz with the vinegar, sugar and basil in a food processor. Pour through a sieve into a saucepan, rubbing with the back of a ladle. Cook, uncovered, for about 10 minutes until reduced by half. Mix in the cream and simmer for a minute or two, then whisk in the diced butter until nice and smooth. Season and set aside.

4 Divide the lettuces into leaves, discarding the core. Heat the remaining oil and sauté the leaves for about 2 minutes until wilted. Season and set aside.

5 Heat a heavy-based non-stick frying pan and, when hot, add the salmon fillets, skinned side down. Turn the heat to medium and cook for 3–4 minutes. Season the fish as it cooks. Turn the fillets over carefully and cook the other side for 2–3 minutes until the fish feels lightly springy. Season again.

6 To serve, dress the salad with the vinaigrette and place in the centre of four dinner plates. (In the restaurant we mould it neatly in a plain scone cutter.) Arrange the wilted lettuce on top and then the salmon. Serve the sauce around.

Poached wild salmon with Gewürztraminer sauce

Wild salmon has a leaner texture, darker colour and finer flavour than farmed salmon, purely because it grows in a totally natural ocean environment – swimming in strong currents and feeding on a completely wild diet. Yet ironically it cannot be classified as 'organic' because governing bodies cannot guarantee the origin of its feed. In season from February through to August, you will find the price reflects the prime quality. A rich fish, salmon suits sweet wine sauces, especially the spicy Alsace Gewürztraminer wine. Serve with blanched and buttery wild asparagus and an accompaniment of baby new Maris Piper potatoes and broccoli florets in an almondy-butter dressing. **SERVES 4**

4 *darnes* of wild salmon (cutlets from
   the middle of the fish with a central
   bone and skin), about 150g each
Court bouillon (page 184), for poaching
120g wild or thin asparagus spears
a little melted butter
sea salt and freshly ground black pepper

Sauce
300ml Gewürztraminer wine
300ml Fish stock (page 184)
3 tablespoons double cream
25g butter

1 Make sure the salmon is clean and free of any blood in the cavity region. Bring the court bouillon to a gentle boil, then slip in the *darnes*. Remove from the heat and leave the fish to cook in the residual heat for 10 minutes.

2 Meanwhile, to make the sauce, boil the wine and stock together until reduced down by half to 300ml. Whisk in the cream and butter, and check the seasoning.

3 Blanch the asparagus in boiling water for 2 minutes, then drain and refresh in ice-cold water. Drain again, then place in a small saucepan with a little melted butter ready for reheating.

4 Remove the fish from the bouillon when it feels firm. Carefully pull out the central bones and gently peel away the skin. Lay the *darnes* on warmed dinner plates.

5 Briefly reheat the asparagus in the melted butter, then place over the salmon. Spoon over a little sauce and strain the rest into a sauceboat to hand round separately.

Wild brown trout with a lemon and caviar sabayon

I adore fishing, and sneak out to beaches or river banks whenever I can. From May to August is the mayfly season, so I head down to the river Kennet near Hungerford and cast my line with a mayfly bait (sprayed with oil to help it float). When I land brown trout, this is how I like to cook and serve them at home, with a classically simple light and eggy sabayon flavoured with lemon and a spoon of Osietra caviar. Baby new potatoes and fresh peas are the best accompaniments.
SERVES 4

2 wild brown trout, about 1kg each
2 large globe artichokes
a squeeze of lemon juice
a little olive oil, for frying
a good knob of butter
sea salt and freshly ground black pepper

Sabayon
6 free-range egg yolks
1 teaspoon lemon juice
grated zest of 1 small lemon
1 tablespoon Osietra caviar

1 Fillet the trout, leaving the skin on. (Or ask your fishmonger to do this.) Check the flesh for pinbones with your fingertips and pull out with tweezers or thin pliers. Score the skin several times in even cuts using the tip of a razor-sharp knife. Set aside.

2 Cut off the artichoke stalks, pull off the leaves and cut out the hairy choke, to leave the hearts. Cook the hearts in boiling salted water with a good squeeze of lemon juice for about 15 minutes. Drain and cool, then cut into diamonds or slices.

3 Fry the pieces of artichoke heart in a little oil and butter until nicely browned. Drain and keep warm.

4 Preheat the grill. Meanwhile, make the sabayon. Whisk the yolks, lemon juice, 1 tablespoon water and seasoning in a bowl set over a pan of simmering water until the mixture triples in volume and becomes light and frothy. (Best to do this with a hand-held electric mixer.) Remove the bowl from the water and set aside whilst you cook the trout.

5 Brush the trout skin with a little oil and grill for about 4 minutes to crisp the skin. Turn over, season the flesh and brush with more oil. Return to the grill and cook for a few more minutes until just browned. Reduce the heat to low and continue cooking until the trout feels just firm but still springy when pressed, 4–5 more minutes.

6 Return the bowl of sabayon to the simmering water and whisk quickly to froth up. Then off the heat fold in the lemon zest and caviar.

7 Dish the fish on to four warmed plates, arrange the artichoke pieces around and spoon the sauce over the top. Serve immediately.

Cod with crispy potatoes and mustard lentils

Fish, potatoes and pulses are natural partners – think of fish and chips with mushy peas. This is a more sophisticated variation, using the waxy Belle Fontaine potatoes and dainty Puy lentils. A terrific light winter main course. **SERVES 4**

400g even-sized Belle Fontaine
  potatoes, scrubbed
4 tablespoons olive oil
4 fillets of cod, about 125g each, with skin
100g Puy lentils
1 carrot
½ small onion
1 small stick celery

15g butter
1 shallot, finely chopped
1 tablespoon capers, rinsed and patted dry
2 tablespoons Vinaigrette (page 184)
  mixed with 1 teaspoon Dijon mustard
1 tablespoon chopped fresh chives
sea salt and freshly ground black pepper

1 Cook the potatoes in boiling salted water for about 12 minutes until just tender. Drain and cool until you can handle them – they are best peeled hot (we put on rubber gloves). Cut into neat dice and toss with 1 tablespoon of the oil. Spread out on a tray, season and let the potatoes absorb the oil as they cool.

2 Season the skin side of the cod with salt, rubbing it in nicely. Leave for half an hour. This helps to dry out the skin.

3 Place the lentils in a saucepan with the carrot, onion and celery. Cover with cold water and bring to the boil. Simmer for about 15 minutes or until just cooked. Do not overcook or the lentils will break down. Drain immediately and discard the vegetables. Spread the lentils on a tray to cool. This stops them cooking further.

4 When ready to cook, heat 1 tablespoon of the oil with the butter in a frying pan, and gently sauté the shallot for about 5 minutes. Scoop out the shallot and reserve. Add another tablespoon of oil to the pan, raise the heat and tip in the diced potato. Cook until nicely golden brown, turning as necessary. Remove, mix with the shallot and capers, and keep warm.

5 Wipe out the pan and heat the remaining tablespoon of oil in it. When hot, add the fish, skin side down. Cook until the skin crisps up nicely (make sure the heat isn't too high or the skin will burn). I always cook my cod for 90% of the total time on the skin side, then flip over just to brown the other side lightly. Cooking time depends on the thickness of the fillet, but is about 5 minutes in all. Check if the fish is cooked by pressing with the back of a fork. It should be lightly springy.

6 Reheat the lentils briefly in a saucepan, season and stir in the vinaigrette and chives. Sit a cod fillet on each of four warmed plates, and spoon over the lentils and then the potatoes. Serve hot.

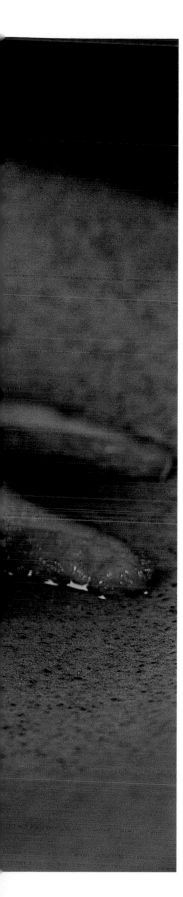

Roasted cod with garlic pomme purée

Chunky cod with creamed potatoes is one of our national culinary treasures, especially if cooked perfectly. Cod fillets from a fish about 4–5kg in weight give perfect texture – any larger and the flakes of flesh become too big and won't hold together after cooking. Did you know cod is the fish with the least amount of scales? This means the skin can be scored easily. We take advantage of this and insert 'cloutes' of herbs – thyme or rosemary sprigs or rolled-up basil leaves – through the skin. For the garlic potato, blanch and refresh the garlic cloves at least three times so you get the flavour without pungency. **SERVES 4**

2 large potatoes (such as Desirée
   or Maris Piper)
6 large cloves garlic
150ml milk
4 tablespoons double cream
75g butter
100g large fresh ceps, trimmed
   and thinly sliced

juice of ¹⁄₂ lemon
1 tablespoon olive oil
4 large *tranches* of cod (thick, neat
   pieces of fillet), 175–200g each, skin on
sea salt and freshly ground black pepper

1 Peel the potatoes and cut into even-size dice. Cook in boiling salted water for 12–15 minutes. Drain well, then return to the pan and dry out for 1–2 minutes over the heat. Mash the flesh or press through a potato ricer back into the pan.

2 While the potatoes are cooking, blanch the garlic in boiling water for a minute, then drain and refresh in cold water. Repeat the blanching twice more, then peel off the skin and mash the cloves to a purée on a small plate using a saucer. Mix into the potato.

3 Scald the milk and slowly stir into the potato purée with some seasoning. Then slowly add the cream to make a nice, velvety smooth purée. Cook out gently for 5 minutes, then gradually beat in half the butter which has been cut into small dice.

4 Meanwhile, heat the remaining butter in a saucepan and gently fry the ceps for about 4 minutes. Add the lemon juice and toss well until piping hot.

5 Heat the oil in a heavy-based frying pan and add the fish, skin side down. Cook for 6–7 minutes until just firm, then flip the *tranches* over and cook briefly on the other side – 90% of the cooking time should be on the skin side.

6 To serve, place the pomme purée in the middle of four dinner plates, set the cod on top and scatter the ceps around.

Roast turbot with asparagus velouté

Turbot is one of the largest of the flat fish, with flesh that is both tender and quite meaty. Chefs love it because it is so accommodating and teams well with a variety of flavours. This is a lovely dish with which to welcome spring to your table, chic and yet quite casual in presentation.

SERVES 4

600g fillet of turbot, skinned

250g fresh green asparagus

3 tablespoons olive oil

1 shallot, chopped

leaves from 1 sprig fresh tarragon, chopped

300ml Fish stock (page 184)

about 50g fresh baby leaf spinach

2 tablespoons double cream

200g tagliatelle (preferably fresh)

25g butter

1 tablespoon chopped fresh chives

sea salt and freshly ground black pepper

1 Cut the fish across into four even slices and trim to neaten. Set aside.

2 Trim the bases of the asparagus spears and peel the stalks, if necessary. Chop half of the spears into small pieces; reserve the other half.

3 Heat 1 tablespoon of the oil and sauté the chopped asparagus gently with the shallot and tarragon for 5 minutes. Add half the stock and a little seasoning, and simmer, uncovered, for 3–5 minutes until tender. Add the spinach and cook until wilted.

4 Whiz the asparagus and spinach mixture in a blender or food processor until smooth. Pass through a sieve into a saucepan, rubbing with the back of a ladle. Mix in the cream and set aside until ready to serve.

5 Cook the tagliatelle in boiling salted water until just *al dente*. Drain, rinse under cold water and drain again. Return to the pan with half of the butter. Set aside. (This is what we do in the restaurant, but you may prefer to cook the pasta later, while you are cooking the fish.)

6 Cook the remaining asparagus in lightly salted boiling water for about 3 minutes until just tender. Drain, rinse under cold water, drain again and return to the pan with the remaining butter.

7 Heat the remaining oil in a large non-stick frying pan and, when hot, cook the fish for about 1 minute on each side until nicely coloured. Season the fish as it cooks. Pour in the remaining stock and bubble gently, spooning the pan juices over the fish. This part-braising keeps the fish moist. After about 3 minutes the stock should have reduced to a syrupy glaze and the fish will be just tender.

8 Heat the pasta, adding a splash of water if necessary to stop it from sticking. Season and toss in the chives. Reheat the asparagus spears.

9 Place the pasta in the centre of four warmed plates. Meanwhile, reheat the asparagus and spinach velouté. Centre the fish on top of the pasta, spoon around the hot velouté and surround with the blanched asparagus spears. Serve quickly.

Turbot with courgette flower fritters and Noilly Prat sauce

When courgette flowers are in season, I like to dip them in a light beer batter and fry them, holding them down with a spatula in the hot oil so they cook flat. These go on top of fillets of turbot, served on a bed of wilted spinach with a Noilly Prat velouté. **SERVES 4**

4 courgette flowers, still with
  tiny whole courgettes attached
120ml tepid milk
75g plain flour, plus extra for dusting
1 teaspoon easy-blend dried yeast
1 teaspoon beer
1 medium courgette, cut into small even dice
light olive oil, for frying
4 fillets of turbot, about 125g each,
  skinned (ideally cut in *tranche* shapes)
15g butter
250ml Fish stock (page 184)
120g baby leaf spinach

Sauce
2 shallots, chopped
10g butter
100ml dry white wine
120ml Noilly Prat
250ml Fish stock (page 184)
1 teaspoon chopped fresh tarragon
200ml double cream
a squeeze of lemon juice
sea salt and freshly ground black
  pepper

1 First, make the sauce. Sauté the shallots in the butter for 5 minutes until softened. Pour in the wine and Noilly Prat and cook until reduced to a syrupy consistency. Add the fish stock and tarragon. Boil until reduced by half. Add the cream and boil until reduced by half again. Check the seasoning, add a squeeze of lemon juice and pass through a sieve into a clean pan. Set aside.

2 Now, for the flowers. Split the tiny courgettes (still attached to the flowers) up the middle. Whisk the milk with the flour, yeast, beer and a good pinch of salt. Set aside.

3 Lightly sauté the diced courgette in a little hot oil until lightly coloured. Season and drain on kitchen paper towel. Preheat the oven to 200°C, Gas 6.

4 Heat a tablespoon of oil in a non-stick frying pan (with an ovenproof handle) and, when hot, fry the turbot until it caramelises nicely on one side. Slide in the butter and carefully flip the fish over. Pour in the fish stock. Cover with a butter paper and transfer to the oven to cook for about 7 minutes, basting once with the stock. Remove the fish and allow to stand.

5 Now back to the courgette flowers. Toss them with a little flour. Heat 2cm depth of oil in a deep frying pan to about 180°C. When it is hot, dip a flower into the batter, press open the tiny courgette and slip it gently into the hot oil. Using a spatula, hold the courgette open if possible so it cooks flat. Cook for a minute or two until golden brown, then remove and drain. Repeat with the other flowers.

6 To serve, make sure your plates are very hot, and press the spinach leaves into the centre of each, so they wilt. Drain the turbot and put a fillet on each mound of spinach. Reheat the diced courgette in a small pan and sprinkle over. Reheat the sauce and nappé the fish with a little; serve the rest separately in a little jug. Finally, top the fish with the courgette flowers.

John Dory with ratatouille vegetables and white beans

We tend to think of aubergines, peppers and courgettes as early autumn vegetables – grown naturally, they are in abundance at this time of year. I 'marry' them with some nicely cooked haricot beans, then serve with some pan-fried fillets of John Dory. This fish is best cooked with its skin on – the flesh parts into three segments, so the skin is necessary to hold the fillets together. The sauce is made with chicken stock. I often serve meat stocks with full-flavoured fish. Incidentally, you can cook double or even treble the amount of beans and freeze what you don't use. It makes sound kitchen sense to cook a larger batch. **SERVES 4**

100g dried haricot beans,
  soaked overnight
½ small onion
1 small carrot, halved
2 sprigs fresh thyme
1 aubergine
2 medium courgettes
4 red peppers

4 yellow peppers
3 tablespoons olive oil
500ml Dark chicken stock (page 184)
150ml double cream
4 fillets of John Dory, about 120g each,
  skin on
sea salt and freshly ground black pepper

1 Drain the soaked beans and place in a pan of cold water. Bring to the boil and boil steadily for 10 minutes. Then drain and cover with fresh cold water. Add the onion, carrot and 1 sprig of thyme. Bring to the boil, then simmer for 45–55 minutes until the beans are just tender but still whole. Drain, and discard the onion, carrot and thyme. Season the beans as they cool.

2 Cut off the skin of the aubergine in 1.5cm thick lengths. You want nicely coloured strips of vegetable, with skin. Discard the inner flesh or use it elsewhere. Cut the aubergine strips into triangles about 2.5cm on all sides. Do the same with the courgettes.

3 Peel the skin from the whole peppers using a swivel vegetable peeler. Cut off the flesh in long pieces and discard the cores. Cut the pepper flesh into triangles too.

4 Heat 2 tablespoons of the oil in a frying pan and gently sauté the aubergines for about 3 minutes. Add the peppers and sauté for 2 minutes, then add the courgettes and sauté for a further 2–3 minutes. Season nicely. Ladle in about 100ml of the stock, and add a few of the remaining thyme leaves. Simmer uncovered until the liquid reduces right down and coats the vegetables in a glossy glaze. Stir in the haricots and reheat gently.

5 While the vegetables are cooking, boil the remaining stock until reduced by half. Add the cream and the last of the thyme leaves, and cook for 5 minutes. Season to taste.

6 Finally, heat the last of the oil in a large non stick frying pan. Season the fish and cook it on the skin side for 3 minutes until nicely browned. Carefully turn the fillets over and cook the other side for 2 minutes or until just firm but still a little springy.

7 Divide the vegetables among four warmed plates, sit a fish fillet on top of each and pour the sauce around.

Monkfish with creamy curried mussels

This is a chunky, yet light and creamy main meal 'soup', perfect for a blustery day when you'd like a dish of warming comfort food. The monkfish fillets are dusted in curry spices before roasting, which gives them an appetising colour and crust. **SERVES** 4

1 large tail of monkfish, 450–500g,
  filleted in two

250g mussels

1 bay leaf

1 sprig fresh thyme

50ml dry white wine

1 carrot, finely diced

1 small leek, finely diced

1 small stick celery, finely diced

2 tablespoons olive oil

2 teaspoons mild curry powder

2 pinches of saffron strands, crushed

300ml Noilly Prat

300ml Fish stock (page 184)

300ml double cream

100g baby leaf spinach, shredded

sea salt and freshly ground black pepper

1 Trim off as much of the grey membrane from the monkfish as possible. (It is important to do this so the fish does not curl during cooking.) Cut each fillet in half lengthways so you have four fillets about 100g each. Set aside and chill.

2 Scrub the mussels and remove beards, if necessary. Discard any that don't close when tapped. Heat a large pan until very hot, then tip in the mussels with the thyme and wine. Clamp on the lid and cook for 3–4 minutes, shaking the pan once or twice. Uncover and discard any mussels that are still closed. Strain off the juices and reserve. Remove the mussel meat from the shells.

3 Sauté the diced carrot, leek and celery (*mirepoix*) in 1 tablespoon of the oil for about 5 minutes until softened. Add 1 teaspoon of the curry powder and the saffron and cook for a few seconds, then pour in the Noilly Prat. Cook until reduced right down to a syrupy consistency. Add the stock and reserved mussel juices and cook until reduced by half. Stir in the cream and simmer for 5 minutes. Season nicely and mix in the mussels and spinach. Reheat and keep the 'soup' hot.

4 Dust the monkfish fillets with salt and the remaining curry powder. Heat the remaining oil in a non-stick frying pan and, when nice and hot, sear the fish in the hot oil, turning to brown evenly. Cook for 3–4 minutes on each side until the flesh firms enough to feel just lightly springy when pressed with the back of a fork. Season again. Remove and allow to rest for 3–4 minutes, then slice into medallions if you like.

5 Divide the 'soup' among four warmed soup plates. Arrange the monkfish on top and serve hot.

Roasted sea bass with chive crème fraîche, baby potatoes and artichokes

This dish is so simple and so fresh. Wild sea bass, reared and caught naturally, has a greater depth of flavour than farmed. It also has a firmer texture because the fish swim against tides and currents and so develop leaner muscle. Match it with other summer favourites – firm waxy new potatoes and fresh artichoke hearts or crisp green beans. **SERVES 4**

2 large globe artichokes
1 tablespoon lemon juice
500g new potatoes (such as
  Jersey Royals)
2 tablespoons chopped fresh chives
100g thick crème fraîche
6 tablespoons olive oil
1 tablespoon shredded fresh basil

100ml Vinaigrette (page 184)
2 shallots, finely chopped
1 tablespoon sherry vinegar
2 tablespoons double cream
800g fillet of sea bass, trimmed
  and cut into 4 neat portions, skin on
sprigs fresh thyme, to garnish
sea salt and freshly ground black pepper

1 Cut off the artichoke stalks, pull off the leaves and cut out the hairy choke, leaving you with just the cup-shaped meaty hearts. Cut the hearts into lengths and then into diamond shapes.
2 Cook the pieces of artichoke in boiling water with the lemon juice for 10 minutes until barely tender; drain. At the same time, boil the new potatoes in another pan until only just tender; drain when they are ready, then cut them in half.
3 Meanwhile, mix the chives into the crème fraîche and season nicely. Set aside.
4 Heat 2 tablespoons of the oil in a frying pan and sauté the potatoes for about 5 minutes until nicely coloured. Remove with a slotted spoon and drain on kitchen paper towel. Beat the basil into the vinaigrette, then mix with the warm potatoes and leave to cool.
5 Add the artichokes to the frying pan, with another tablespoon of oil if necessary, and sauté for 3–5 minutes until nicely coloured. Remove with a slotted spoon, drain and keep warm.
6 Add the shallots to the pan and sauté for 5 minutes until softened. Deglaze with the vinegar and cook until the liquid has reduced away. Stir in the cream, season and set aside to keep warm.
7 Score the skin of the bass several times with the tip of a very sharp knife. Heat the remaining oil in a large frying pan. Season the bass and cook, skin side down, for 3–4 minutes until the silver skin is crispy. Turn carefully and cook the other side for 1–2 minutes until lightly springy when pressed. Season again.
8 To serve, spoon the artichokes in the centre of four warmed plates. Spoon the shallot cream on top. Sit the sea bass on this, arrange the basil potatoes around the fish and garnish with thyme. Finally, spoon the chive crème fraîche on top so it melts invitingly over the fish as you serve.

Brill in red wine with beurre rouge

You may find it strange cooking white fish in red wine, but it works really well and looks so attractive when you cut into the fillet. The sauce, called a beurre rouge, is made by reducing the liquor down and whisking in butter. Vegetable accompaniments include potato purée, butter-glazed grelot onions (or baby shallots) and salsify. **SERVES 4**

500g potatoes (such as Desirée)

5 tablespoons double cream

150g butter, plus a good knob

150g salsify

a good squeeze of lemon juice

3 tablespoons olive oil

12 grelot onions, peeled

1 large shallot, finely chopped

500ml red wine

500ml Fish stock (page 184)

4 fillets of brill, about 150g each

1 tablespoon chopped fresh parsley

sea salt and fresh ground black pepper

1 Cook the potatoes, in their skins, in boiling salted water for 12–15 minutes until tender, then drain. Peel whilst hot (wear rubber gloves), then mash or press through a potato ricer back into the pan. Heat for a minute or two, then beat in 3 tablespoons of the cream and 25g of the butter until thick and creamy. Season and set aside.

2 Peel the salsify with a swivel peeler, then rinse well and slice diagonally into thin bâtons. Blanch in boiling water with the lemon juice for 2 minutes, then drain and cool.

3 Heat 2 tablespoons of the oil and, when hot, sauté the onions for about 5 minutes, turning frequently. Pat the salsify dry, then add to the pan with the knob of butter. Cook for a few more minutes until nicely coloured. Set aside and keep warm.

4 Heat the remaining oil in a medium saucepan and gently sauté the shallot for 5 minutes. Pour in the wine and stock, and bring to a gentle simmer.

5 Trim the brill fillets to neaten, and season them. Slip into the hot liquid. Poach the fish for 3–4 minutes until just tender. Do not overcook. Remove the fish with a fish slice and keep warm.

6 Strain the fish liquor through a fine sieve, then return to the pan. Boil rapidly until reduced by two-thirds, then stir in the remaining cream and some seasoning. Bring back to a gentle boil, then, on a low heat, whisk in the remaining butter, cut in small cubes, adding them one or two at a time. The sauce will thicken slightly and become glossy. Watch carefully that it doesn't 'split'.

7 Reheat the potato purée and divide among four warmed plates. Sit a brill fillet on top of each mound of potatoes and arrange the glazed vegetables around. Nappé with the sauce, sprinkle with parsley and serve.

Saffron red mullet on vegetables à la grecque

Red mullet, as you may have gathered, is one of my favourite foods. It not only tastes good, the thin red skin looks so inviting, and it gives me great scope to cook it in so many ways. You will need small fishes if possible for this recipe, or failing that two larger ones about 500g each, with fillets cut in half. The fish is served on vegetables in a spicy oil marinade – a great casual main meal. The same idea works well with very fresh mackerel. Grelots are squat onions popular in France. Tubby shallots will do if you can't find them. **SERVES 4**

4 small red mullets, about 250g each,
   neatly filleted in two, skin on
5 tablespoons olive oil
2 generous pinches of saffron strands
4 baby fennels, or 2 medium ones
2 medium carrots, thinly sliced
8 grelot onions or 4 fat shallots, sliced
sea salt and freshly ground black pepper

Marinade
150ml olive oil
1 tablespoon white wine vinegar
1 tablespoon aged balsamic vinegar
6 coriander seeds, roughly crushed
6 white peppercorns, roughly crushed
1–4 star anise
4 whole cloves
6 sprigs fresh coriander

1 Heat all the ingredients for the marinade until on the point of boiling, then set aside to infuse for 10–15 minutes.

2 Meanwhile, prepare the mullets. Trim the fillets neatly, feeling for any pin bones with the tips of your fingers and pulling them out with tweezers or your fingernails. (If the fillets are large, then cut each across in two.) Rub both sides with 2 tablespoons of the olive oil and season. Crush the saffron strands on top of the pretty pink skin side. Set aside to marinate for 5–10 minutes.

3 If using baby fennel, trim and cut each in half lengthways. If using larger bulbs, cut into quarters. Sauté the fennel in the remaining 3 tablespoons of olive oil for 3–5 minutes, then add the carrots and sauté for 2 minutes. Finally, add the onions (or shallots) and sauté for a further 2 minutes. Remove the vegetables to a shallow serving dish, season and pour over the marinade. Leave to cool to room temperature.

4 Heat a large non-stick frying pan and, when you can feel a good heat rising, place the

fillets in, saffron-crusted skin side down. Cook on this side for 5 minutes until the flesh
feels nearly firm and the skin is nice and crispy. Carefully flip the fillets over, taking care
not to tear the skin, and cook the other side for a minute or two. Season well.

5 Slip each cooked fillet gently into the dish and spoon over the vegetables and marinade
to cover. Cool the fish to room temperature. Carefully pour off the marinade. (The marinade
can be strained and stored in the fridge for up to a week to be used again.)

6 Serve the mullet fillets and marinated vegetables at room temperature or lightly chilled.
This dish is good with a lightly dressed rocket salad.

Red mullet with orange-glazed fennel and pesto dressing

Fennel is a popular vegetable all over the Mediterranean – market stalls and farmers' carts are often piled high with crisp, fresh bulbs, full of juicy aniseed flavour. Our use of it is often restricted to salads or, occasionally, cooking with a tomato sauce. But there are many other flavours of the sun it complements. Orange is one, pesto another and, of course, it is one of the great fish accompaniments. This meal combines all these elements. **SERVES 4**

4 medium red mullets, 250–300g each,
   neatly filleted in two, skin on
2 good pinches of saffron strands,
   finely crushed
3 tablespoons Vinaigrette (page 184)
2 large bulbs fennel
4 tablespoons olive oil
1 teaspoon fine sea salt
1 teaspoon caster sugar
200ml fresh orange juice

15g butter
sea salt and freshly ground black pepper

Pesto
25g pine kernels
2 fat cloves garlic, roughly chopped
15g leaves fresh basil
50g Parmesan cheese, freshly grated
3 tablespoons extra virgin olive oil

1 Neaten the edges of the mullet fillets. Check the flesh for pin bones and pull them out. Rub the crushed saffron over the pink skin. Set aside in the fridge.

2 Make the pesto in a food processor, whizzing all the ingredients together. Mix with the vinaigrette. Set aside.

3 To prepare the fennel, trim the tops, then using a small sharp knife, shave off the rough ribs. Cut each bulb in half lengthways. Cut out the core, but leave the root end intact, to hold the layers together.

4 Preheat the oven to 190°C, Gas 5. Heat 2 tablespoons of the oil in a large flameproof pan that can be used in the oven. Mix the salt and sugar together and sprinkle over the fennel. Add the fennel halves to the pan, pressing them firmly into the hot oil, and turn once or twice to colour them well all over. Deglaze with the orange juice and slip the knob of butter down the side of the pan. Spoon the juices over the fennel.

5 Cover with a butter paper and transfer to the oven. Cook for 15–20 minutes until the fennel is softened, basting at least twice with the pan juices. Check the tenderness with the tip of a sharp knife.

6 While the fennel is cooking, heat the remaining 2 tablespoons of oil in a large heavy-based pan and fry the mullet fillets for a good 3 minutes on the skin side. Carefully flip the fillets over and cook the other side briefly, about 1 minute. Mullet is a delicate fish, so treat it carefully. Remove and keep warm.

7 Lift the fennel halves on to a board. Make neat cuts from root to tip, keeping the root uncut so it keeps the fennel halves together. Transfer to warmed plates and press the 'fans' open. Lay two mullet fillets on top of each fennel fan and drizzle around the pesto dressing.

Baby red mullets with choucroute and rhubarb

Little red mullets are filleted into a butterfly shape, then marinated and pan-fried. These are served on a salad that might make you gasp – choucroute with celery and rhubarb dressed with pink grapefruit vinaigrette. It has to be tried to be believed! Baby new potatoes and blanched spinach are good accompaniments. **SERVES 4**

4 small red mullets, about 200g each

3 tablespoons olive oil

2 pinches of saffron strands, crushed

4 sticks pink rhubarb, trimmed

4 inner sticks of celery, trimmed

100g choucroute (sauerkraut)
   from a jar, rinsed in cold water

150ml Vegetable nage (page 184)

15g butter

1 pink grapefruit

5 tablespoons Vinaigrette (page 184)

leaves from 2 sprigs fresh coriander, shredded

sea salt and freshly ground black pepper

1 Cut the heads from the mullets, then, using kitchen scissors, cut along the belly of each fish and gut. Wash the cavity well under cold running water, rubbing away any blood spots. Lay the fish on a board and slit down to the tail end. Using the tip of a sharp filleting knife, loosen the backbone and finer bones from the flesh on both sides, then snip the bones carefully from the skin and discard. You want to fillet the fish, keeping the two sides joined together to form a butterfly shape.

2 Pat the fish dry. Brush both sides with 1 tablespoon of the olive oil. Crush the saffron over the pink skins and rub in. Chill uncovered for 2 hours.

3 Meanwhile, make the choucroute salad. Cut the rhubarb and celery into thin bâtons 4cm long. Sweat the choucroute in the rest of the oil for 3 minutes, then add the rhubarb and celery. Cook for a further 2 minutes. Pour in the nage and seasoning. Dot with the butter and place a butter paper on top. Turn the heat right down and simmer very gently for 10 minutes, basting once or twice.

4 Meanwhile, peel the grapefruit, removing all white pith, and cut out the segments from the membrane. Break up the grapefruit segments in a bowl with a fork into little pink 'tears'. Mix with the vinaigrette.

5 Remove the choucroute from the heat and mix in half the grapefruit vinaigrette. Check the seasoning. Allow to cool to room temperature, then toss in the coriander.

6 When ready to serve, heat a large non-stick frying pan and, when hot, fry the mullets for 3–4 minutes on the skin side until crisp. Flip them over carefully and cook briefly on the other side. Do not overcook, as the fish are small and delicate.

7 Divide the salad among four plates and place a pretty fish on top of each. Glaze with the rest of the grapefruit vinaigrette and serve.

Whiting with a lemon and parsley crust

I think whiting is an underrated fish, eclipsed by the meatier cod and haddock. But although the flesh of whiting is more tender, the flavour is good. This recipe suits large size whiting, which your fishmonger should be able to fillet into four neat long fillets. The crust is made in an ingenious way. Instead of pressing a loose mass on to each fillet, it is pressed together as a sheet, cut and placed on top. Then the fish is cooked half submerged in liquid, with the crust poking out at the top. To complete the fresh green theme, you could serve the fish on a mound of baby leaf spinach. Just place the spinach on piping hot plates so the leaves wilt – no need to cook. SERVES 4

1 large whiting, about 1.2kg,
   filleted in four, skin on

3 tomatoes, skinned, seeded
   and finely chopped

3 tablespoons olive oil

3 tablespoons coarsegrain mustard

1 bay leaf

2 sprigs fresh thyme

3 tablespoons double cream

sea salt and freshly ground black pepper

Crust

200g unsalted butter

200g unsweetened brioche crumbs
   or good-quality white breadcrumbs

100g curly-leaf parsley sprigs

grated zest of 2 lemons

1 Check the fillets for any pinbones, then cut each across in two to make 8 pieces. Set aside.

2 Cook the chopped tomato in 1 tablespoon of the olive oil until you have a slightly chunky purée. Season and set aside.

3 Make the crust. Blend the butter and crumbs in a food processor until crumbly. Drop in the parsley, lemon zest and seasoning, and whiz to fine crumbs. Line a wooden board with cling film and tip the buttery crumb mixture on top. Cover with more cling film, and roll out with a rolling pin to a rectangle about 1cm thick. Place this crust in the freezer to firm up for a couple of hours. Then cut into 8 pieces about the same size as the fish fillets.

4 When ready to cook, preheat the oven to 200°C, Gas 6. Spread 2 tablespoons of the mustard over the skin of the fish, then spoon on the tomato 'purée'. Finally, lift the crust cut-outs off the film and press gently on top. Lay gently in a flameproof baking dish, crust side up.

5 Put the remaining oil in a small saucepan with about 300ml of water, the herbs and seasoning. Bring to the boil. Pour the liquid down the side of the baking dish so it doesn't wet the crust. Bake, uncovered, for 8–10 minutes until the crust is light and crisp and the fish feels firm when pressed lightly in the centre. Remove from the heat and, using a long spatula, lift out the fish on to four warmed dinner plates.

6 Place the baking dish on the hob and boil down the liquid by half, then add the remaining mustard and the cream. Pour neatly around the fish. Serve with baby new potatoes.

Spring chickens with baby pak choi in sweet-sour sauce

Oriental flavours have been enthusiastically embraced in classic European kitchens – it's all about culinary lateral thinking. I like to serve roasted poussins (aka spring chickens) with a sweet-sour sauce and tiny heads of Chinese 'spring greens' called pak choi, which are now grown commercially in European market gardens. Don't trim the pak choi – they are cooked whole. **SERVES 4**

4 tablespoons olive oil

4 poussins, 500–600g each

75g butter, melted

8 heads small pak choi

2 tablespoons dark soy sauce

sea salt and freshly ground black pepper

Sauce

1 red pepper, chopped

1 yellow pepper, chopped

1 tablespoon olive oil

1 tablespoon white wine vinegar

1 teaspoon caster sugar

3 tablespoons Vinaigrette (page 184)

1 First, make the sauce. Sauté the chopped peppers in the oil for about 5 minutes until softened. Deglaze with the vinegar and add the sugar, stirring until dissolved. Whiz to a fine purée in a blender or food processor with the vinaigrette. Rub through a sieve with the back of a ladle. Season and set aside.

2 Preheat the oven to 200°C, Gas 6. Heat 2 tablespoons of the oil in a large frying pan. When hot, add the birds, two at a time, and brown all over. (In the restaurant we press the poussins down with our hands so they colour evenly, but this is only for the brave – or foolhardy!)

3 Place the birds in a roasting tin, open out their legs and trickle over the melted butter, pouring it through a small sieve. Season. Roast for 15–20 minutes, basting the birds at least twice – spoon up the pan juices and trickle them through the sieve again. This gives the poussins an evenly golden, crisp skin. Spoon the juices inside the birds as well if possible, for flavour. When cooked, remove from the oven and set aside to rest.

4 You can serve the birds whole, or you can serve them like this: using a very sharp knife, remove the breasts from the bone in one piece. Cut through the thigh joint and remove the legs. We then loosen and pull out the thigh bone, leaving the drumstick, but you may find this just too much trouble! Discard the carcasses. Keep the meat warm.

5 Trim the pak choi neatly and sauté whole in the remaining oil for about 3 minutes. Deglaze with the soy sauce and season with pepper only.

6 To serve, place the pak choi in the centre of four warmed plates and sit the chicken on top. Reheat the sauce gently and spoon over the chicken. This is nice with butter-dressed tagliatelle.

Grilled chicken with tagliatelle and morel velouté

This is a rustic dish par excellence – wonderful to come home to, or to make for a relaxed dinner party. I suggest chicken breasts (preferably from free-range corn-fed birds), but you could substitute guinea fowl or pheasant breasts. Try to use fresh tagliatelle from a reputable Italian deli. If that is not possible then buy a good-quality dried pasta such as De Cecco or Delverde rather than a supermarket own brand. Italians take their pasta qualities seriously, and so should we. SERVES 4

about 100g fresh morels
3–4 tablespoons olive oil
1 large shallot, finely chopped
150ml dry white wine
500ml Dark chicken stock (page 184)
250ml double cream
500g tagliatelle (preferably fresh)
4 boneless chicken breasts, skin on, about 120g each
sea salt and freshly ground black pepper

1 Cut the morels in half lengthways, then rinse well in cold running water to extract all the sand. Pat dry on kitchen paper towel and leave for 1 hour to dry completely.

2 Trim half of the morels into neat shapes. Chop the rest, with the trimmings, quite finely.

3 Make the sauce ahead, if liked. Heat 1 tablespoon of the oil and gently sauté the shallot until nicely coloured, about 5 minutes. Add the finely chopped morels and continue cooking for 3 minutes. Pour in the wine and cook until reduced by half. Add the stock and season lightly. Boil until reduced by half again, then stir in the cream and simmer for 5 minutes. Pass through a sieve into a clean pan, rubbing with the back of a ladle. Check the seasoning and set aside until ready to serve.

4 Preheat the grill until hot. Brush the chicken skin lightly with a little oil and season. Grill, skin side up, for a few minutes, then lower the heat to medium and continue grilling until the skin becomes nice and crispy. Turn over and cook the other side for a couple of minutes (most of the cooking should be on the skin side). The breasts should be just firm, but not tough.

5 While the chicken is cooking, sauté the trimmed morels in 1 tablespoon of the oil for a few minutes. Make sure they are well roasted or you won't get the best flavour from them. Remove and drain on kitchen paper towel.

6 Cook the pasta in boiling salted water for 3–5 minutes if fresh, or according to pack instructions if dried. Drain, then mix in about half of the sauce and reheat gently. Reheat the remaining sauce.

7 Divide the pasta among four warmed shallow bowls. Cut the chicken into medallions and place on the pasta. Nappé the chicken with the sauce and scatter over the sautéed morels.

Confit of duck legs

There's something very appealing about slow-cooked duck that is meltingly tender and falling away from the bone. I use Gressingham duck, with its slightly lean and full-flavoured meat. You can buy the legs separately, and these are particularly good cooked confit-style in goose fat, then served with chips and a salad of frisée. **SERVES** 4

leaves from 1 sprig fresh thyme
4 duck legs (preferably Gressingham duck)
about 500g goose fat
1 fresh bouquet garni (bay leaf, few
   parsley stalks, sprig fresh thyme and
   a small stick celery tied together)
200g frisée leaves
a little Vinaigrette (page 184)
sea salt and freshly ground black pepper

1 Press the leaves of fresh thyme on to the duck legs and sprinkle with sea salt. Leave at room temperature for 1 hour to draw out some moisture. In the meantime, preheat the oven to 160°C, Gas 3.

2 Put the duck legs and goose fat in a pan and heat gently until just on the point of boiling. Transfer to a shallow casserole and add the bouquet garni. Cover and place in the oven. Slow roast for about 1½ hours until you can loosen the leg bone fairly easily. This indicates the meat is nicely tender.

3 Drain the legs and dab with kitchen paper towel. Strain the fat and keep for sautéeing potatoes and other uses – it is delicious. Heat a dry heavy based frying pan and, when hot, cook the legs skin side down for a few minutes to crisp the skin. Take care not to overcook.

4 Dress the frisée with a little vinaigrette and place in the centre of four plates. Top with the crispy duck legs and serve with sautéed potatoes if you like.

Gressingham duck
with chicory tarts

*Gressingham ducks are one of my favourite things, full of flavour, with a skin that crisps nicely –
as long as you score the skin closely and evenly. The chicory tarts are an unusual accompaniment.
They take a wee while to put together, but they are not difficult. You will need tartlet tins or
large muffin tins for this, 8–10cm diameter and 2–3cm deep.* **SERVES 4**

250g Puff pastry (page 185)

4 medium heads chicory

30g light soft brown sugar

50g butter, plus a good knob

2 tablespoons balsamic vinegar

1 carrot, diced

¼ celeriac, diced

½ small Savoy cabbage, finely shredded

1 tablespoon olive oil

75g smoked lean bacon, cut in small cubes

4 breasts of Gressingham duck, about 175g each

1 tablespoon clear honey

2 whole cloves

sea salt and freshly ground black pepper

1 Roll out the pastry to a 5mm thickness. Cut out four rounds a good 3cm larger than the diameter of your tartlet tins, that is 11–13 cm. Prick the bases lightly and chill to rest. Preheat the oven to 200°C, Gas 6.

2 Using a thin sharp knife, tunnel-core the chicory to remove as much of the hard core as possible, yet still keeping the leaves together. Cut the chicory across so you have the dumpy section from each about 3cm tall. Set aside. (Use the leafy tops in salads.)

3 In a small saucepan, dissolve the sugar in a small sprinkling of water, then add the butter. Melt it, then boil for a minute or so. Mix in the vinegar. Pour this into the tartlet tins. Season the chicory sections, then press one down into the caramel in each tin, cored side up.

4 Fit the pastry discs on top, tucking the edges down inside the tin around the sides. Bake for 12–15 minutes until the pastry is golden brown and crisp. Once or twice during baking, carefully tip out any juices from the tins. The chicory will soften and take on a delicious caramelised flavour. Remove and allow to cool a bit whilst you make the rest of the dish.

5 Blanch the carrot and celeriac in boiling salted water for 3–4 minutes. Add the cabbage and cook for a further 2 minutes. Drain the vegetables and refresh under cold running water; drain well. Wipe out the pan, heat the oil in it and fry the bacon lardons for about 5 minutes, stirring once or twice. Set the pan aside.

6 Trim the duck breasts neatly, then score the skin, taking care not to cut through the fat as well. The closer the scoring lines are together, the crisper the cooked skin. Heat a non-stick heavy-based frying pan and, when hot, put in the duck breasts, skin side down. Cook for a few moments to brown. Fat will seep out. Tip this away so it does not burn. Turn the breasts and brown the flesh side. Season as they cook. Turn once more and baste the flesh side a few times with the pan juices. Cook for a total of 8–10 minutes. Duck is best served slightly pink and juicy.

7 Remove the duck breasts from the pan and keep warm, saving the juices that seep out. Drain off the excess fat from the pan, but hold back the meaty juices. Add the honey and cloves, then

return the duck breasts with their juices, and glaze with the honey mixture. Give the skin side one more turn in the pan to crisp it, then remove the breasts and leave to rest briefly.

8 Meanwhile, reheat the bacon lardons, then add the knob of butter and return the cabbage mixture to the pan. Stir gently until piping hot. Check the seasoning, then spoon in mounds in the centre of four warmed plates. Sit the duck breasts on top (cut into slices diagonally if you like) and trickle over the pan juices. Carefully turn out the chicory tarts, loosening them with a table knife if necessary, and place one on each plate. Using a thin spoon handle or table knife, gently separate the chicory leaves to give a rose effect. Serve immediately.

A quick casserole of pigeon

Casseroles don't have to be cooked long and slow. This one simmers diced winter vegetables in a rich red wine stock and is served with pan-fried breasts of wood pigeon. There's not much meat on a wood pigeon, so I only bother to cook the breasts, serving two for each portion.

SERVES 4

4 nice fat wood pigeons

about 150g salsify

1 small celeriac

1 small swede

2 medium parsnips

4 small red onions or 8 baby ones, peeled

4 tablespoons olive oil

1 sprig fresh rosemary

1 bay leaf

300ml red wine

1 teaspoon tomato purée

1 teaspoon truffle oil

1 litre Dark chicken stock (page 184)

50g mousserons or baby button mushrooms

sea salt and freshly ground black pepper

1 Cut the breasts from the pigeons, so you have two per person. Discard the carcasses (or use to make stock). Set aside.

2 Peel the salsify, celeriac, swede and parsnips, and cut into large dice. If using small rather than baby onions, cut each in half. Heat 1½ tablespoons of the oil in a large pan and tip in all the vegetables including the onions. Toss in the herbs too. Sweat the vegetables for a good 10 minutes so they become nicely coloured.

3 Meanwhile, boil the wine right down until reduced to around 100ml. Stir the tomato purée and the truffle oil into the vegetables, then stir in the wine, stock and some seasoning. Simmer uncovered until the vegetables are just tender, 10–12 minutes. The vegetables should have become wine-stained and the liquid reduced right down.

4 For the pigeons, heat 1½ tablespoons of the remaining oil in a large frying pan. Season the pigeon breasts and quickly fry, skin side down first, for a total of about 6 minutes. The breasts should be lightly springy when pressed and still a little pink inside.

5 Meanwhile, quickly sauté the mousserons in the remaining 1 tablespoon of oil.

6 Divide all the vegetables among four warmed shallow soup plates. Set the pigeon breasts on top, season and serve.

Saddle of rabbit with herb gnocchi

This is a good country dish served with style. Like duck, you can slow-cook rabbit in goose fat until the meat is deliciously tender. Once cooked, the meat can be served with home-made potato gnocchi and some oven-roasted tomatoes. A lovely, lazy lunch course.

SERVES 4

1 saddle of rabbit, about 500g
1 tablespoon olive oil
leaves from 1 sprig fresh rosemary, chopped
400g goose fat
mixed salad leaves, to garnish
sea salt and freshly ground black pepper

Gnocchi
2 large baking potatoes (Desirée or
  Maris Piper), about 400g each
160g plain flour
1 teaspoon fine sea salt
1 large free-range egg
1 tablespoon each chopped fresh basil
  and parsley
3–4 tablespoons olive oil

1 Take the 2 long fillets from the saddle of rabbit. Wrap each tightly in cling film and chill for 24 hours.

2 The next day, unwrap the rabbit fillets and rub lightly with the oil, then sprinkle the surface with a little salt and chopped rosemary leaves. Leave for 1 hour.

3 Place the rabbit and goose fat in a shallow heavy-based saucepan. Bring to the boil, then reduce the heat to the lowest possible – whatever you can get it down to will be okay. Cook for 1–1¼ hours, possibly more, until the meat is tender. Allow the rabbit to cool in the fat, then lift out and dab dry with kitchen paper towel. Keep the fat for other recipes.

4 While the rabbit is cooking, make the gnocchi. Preheat the oven to 180°C, Gas 4. Bake the potatoes for about 1 hour until cooked. (Baking keeps the flesh dry.) Cool, then scoop out the flesh and mash or press through a potato ricer. Mix with the flour, salt, egg and herbs. Gradually work in 3 tablespoons of the oil until you have a firm, but still soft dough.

5 Turn out on to a cold floured surface and knead gently until smooth. Roll into a long cigar shape, wrap in cling film, and allow to rest and cool.

6 Bring a large pan of salted water to the boil and add the remaining oil. Using the back of a table knife (this helps to squash the ends to a traditional gnocchi shape), cut off 3cm lengths. Drop straight into the simmering water and cook for about 3 minutes.

7 Have ready a large bowl of iced water. As each batch of gnocchi is cooked, lift out with a slotted spoon and dunk straight into the iced water. Leave for a minute or so, then drain well and pat dry with kitchen paper towel.

8 When ready to serve, preheat the grill. When it is hot, brown the rabbit fillets lightly on all sides. Meanwhile, heat some oil or goose fat in a frying pan and fry the cooked gnocchi for 3–4 minutes until crispy on both sides. Drain on kitchen paper towel.

9 Cut each rabbit fillet diagonally in half and serve with the gnocchi and a salad leaf garnish.

Escalope of veal with fondant kohlrabi and baby globe artichokes

Winter is a good season for using baby globe artichokes. These are so young the chokes have not yet formed, so can be cooked and eaten whole. Winter is also the time for kohlrabi, with its intriguing turnip-like flavour. If you take time to prepare special vegetable dishes, then it makes sense to serve with a quick-cook cut of meat. My favourite is a slice of 'cushion' of veal (from the top rump), which is called an escalope, although a thin fillet of lamb or pork would do nicely too.

SERVES 4

4 baby globe artichokes
juice of ½ lemon
1 medium kohlrabi, about 500g
25g butter
1 tablespoon olive oil
150ml Light chicken stock (page 184)
4 escalopes of veal, about 100g each
3 tablespoons plain flour
3 tablespoons clarified butter
2 teaspoons chopped fresh chervil
2 teaspoons chopped fresh parsley
2 teaspoons chopped fresh chives
sea salt and freshly ground black pepper

1 First prepare the artichokes. Trim the tips of the leaves and snap off the stalks. Drop into a pan of boiling water with half the lemon juice. Cook for 5 minutes, then drain upside down in a colander. Cool.

2 Peel the kohlrabi and slice into 1.5cm thick rounds. Heat half the butter and the oil in a sauteuse or shallow saucepan. Fry the kohlrabi slices quickly on both sides to brown nicely, then season and pour in the stock. Add half of the remaining butter to the pan and cover with a butter paper. Simmer gently until the stock has evaporated and the slices have softened, 10–12 minutes. Do not turn them. Leave in the pan, but remove from the heat.

3 Now for the veal. Place one of the escalopes between non-stick baking parchment and beat lightly with the flat of a metal cleaver or rolling pin. Don't whack the life out of the meat – just a light battening to flatten and tenderise. Repeat with the other escalopes. Season the flour and toss the veal in it, shaking off any excess.

4 Heat the clarified butter in a heavy-based non-stick frying pan and lay in the veal. Fry quickly for a minute to sear, then slip in the remaining bit of butter. When it froths, turn the veal over. Baste with the frothing butter and cook for 1–2 minutes until the meat feels just firm. Don't overcook. Toss in the chopped herbs, season lightly and squeeze over the remaining lemon juice.

5 Serve the veal on warmed plates. Reheat the artichokes (in a little buttery water) and the kohlrabi, dish with the veal and serve.

Veal rump with a fricassée of ceps and cabbage

This is a good party dish. You can par-cook the vegetables ahead, then reheat while you pan-fry the tender, lean veal rumps just before serving. Veal rumps, which come from the top of the leg, are best marinated for a good 6 hours before cooking. **SERVES 4**

4 steaks of veal rump, about 120g each
4 tablespoons olive oil
1 large bay leaf, crushed
2 sprigs fresh thyme
200g large fresh ceps, bases trimmed
2 medium plum tomatoes, skinned and seeded
1 medium Savoy cabbage
50g butter
2 tablespoons chopped fresh chives
3 tablespoons Vinaigrette (page 184)
sea salt and freshly ground black pepper

1 Trim the veal steaks to neaten, if necessary. Place in a shallow dish and drizzle over half the oil. Tuck the crushed bay leaf and the leaves from 1 thyme sprig between the steaks. Leave to marinate in the fridge for 6 hours.

2 Slice the ceps evenly but not too thinly. Finely chop the tomatoes. Quarter the cabbage, discarding the first layer of outer leaves. Cut out the cabbage core, then shred the leaves finely.

3 Bring a large pan of salted water to the boil and blanch the cabbage for 2 minutes. Drain and refresh under cold running water, then drain well again. Heat the butter in the same pan and add the thyme leaves from the second sprig. Cook for a few seconds, then toss in the blanched cabbage. Stir well and cook for a further 2 minutes until nicely glazed and cooked. Season well, then set aside.

4 Heat the remaining oil in a frying pan and sauté the sliced ceps for about 5 minutes until lightly browned and just tender. Toss in the diced tomato and chives, and season. Mix with the cabbage. Keep hot.

5 Heat a large non-stick frying pan. Lift the veal steaks out of the dish and drain off the oil. Season lightly. Cook the steaks for 2–3 minutes on each side until the meat feels lightly springy when pressed with the back of a fork. Do not overcook – veal should be served 'just above pink'. Remove and allow to rest for a few minutes. Swirl the vinaigrette into the pan to deglaze the juices.

6 To serve, divide the vegetables among four plates. Slice the steaks thinly on the diagonal and arrange on top of the vegetables. Nappé with the pan *jus* and serve.

Ribeye of beef with watercress purée

Ribeye is very much a Scottish cut of beef, which more chefs are beginning to use. It comes from the top end of the sirloin, is a nice round shape, cooks well and – more important – has a great flavour and texture. We buy it in 2-kilo pieces and 'set' the shape by rolling it tightly into a ballotine and storing it in the fridge for 2 days. It can then be cut into thick steaks and grilled or pan-fried. We serve ribeye with an eye-catching watercress purée that is embarrassingly simple to make. (In the restaurant we wring out the watercress purée in a cloth and serve it as a soft quenelle, but if you prefer a pouring sauce then use the maximum amount of cream.) Sit the steaks on a bed of sautéed mushrooms of your choice. I prefer girolles, but you can use ceps, oysters or even the brown champignons de Paris. SERVES 4

600g piece ribeye of beef
3 tablespoons olive oil
15g butter
200g mushrooms (see above), sliced If large
2 fat cloves garlic, finely chopped
2 teaspoons chopped fresh parsley
sea salt and freshly ground black pepper

Sauce
300g watercress
100g spinach leaves
60–200ml double cream

1 First, make the sauce. Put a pan of salted water on to boil. Push in all the watercress and boil for 5 minutes. Add the spinach and cook for another minute or so until wilted. Drain in a colander. Press with the back of a ladle to extract as much moisture as possible.
2 Put the leaves into a food processor and whiz to a fine purée, scraping down the sides occasionally. Pour 60ml of the cream through the processor funnel and keep the blades whirling for what seems like an eternity. You will eventually get a sauce with a texture like silk. It will be so smooth, you will not need to pass it through a sieve. If you want a pouring sauce, add the remaining cream. Check the seasoning, and pour into a small saucepan ready for reheating.
3 Cut the ribeye into 4 even steaks and rub each side using 1 tablespoon oil. Heat a heavy non-stick frying pan until you can feel a good heat rising. Lay in your steaks – they should give a good hiss as they hit the hot pan. Season the tops and cook for about 3 minutes, then flip over and cook the other side for 2 minutes. Slip the butter into the pan at this stage and season the second side. Remove the steaks from the pan and leave to rest while you cook the mushrooms.
4 Sauté the mushrooms with the garlic in the remaining oil. Season and mix with the parsley.
5 Reheat the watercress purée/sauce. Place the steaks on warmed plates (sliced first if you like), trickle over any pan juices and spoon on the mushrooms. If your watercress purée is firm, shape it into quenelles. If it is a sauce, spoon some over the steaks and hand round the rest separately. Serve with chips, sautéed potatoes or slices of warm, fresh baguette.

Braised oxtail with parsnip purée

Oxtail is one of the great British country classic dishes. During the beef ban they weren't available, but now the clusters of oxtail cuts are back in good butchers' shops, and we can enjoy the rich, velvety meat that softens in long, slow cooking. The slices step down in size as the tail narrows. Ideally, you need two good slices per portion. You may find it wise to buy two oxtails and have some leftover for the next day, or to freeze. A comforting parsnip mash is great for soaking up the rich gravy-sauce. This one is a reminder of my first restaurant, the Aubergine. Parsnip purée was so popular, I had to keep it on the menu until I got tired of cooking it. Now, I can reintroduce it. Both elements of this dish can be cooked the day ahead and reheated to serve – another plus in its favour. **SERVES 4**

2 oxtails, about 1kg each, cut in 3cm slices
400ml red wine
1 sprig fresh thyme
1 bay leaf
4 tablespoons olive oil
2 carrots, chopped
1 red onion, chopped
1 litre Dark chicken stock (page 184)
sea salt and freshly ground black pepper

Parsnip purée
4 medium dumpy parsnips
25g butter
1 tablespoon olive oil
1 medium potato, peeled and roughly chopped
300ml Light chicken stock (page 184)
150ml double cream

1 Marinate the oxtails in the wine. The easiest way to do this is to pop the oxtail into a large food bag and pour in the wine and herbs. Seal the bag and rub all together. Store in the fridge overnight.

2 When ready to cook, remove the oxtails and reserve the wine. Heat 2 tablespoons of the olive oil in a large cast-iron casserole and brown the oxtail pieces in succession. Drain on kitchen paper towel.

3 Heat the remaining oil in the pan and sauté the carrots and onion for about 5 minutes until softened. Add the wine marinade (with herbs) and cook until reduced by two-thirds. Pour in the stock and bring to the boil. Return the oxtail pieces and season nicely, then cover and simmer on the gentlest of heats for almost 3 hours until the meat is very tender and falls from the bone when prodded.

4 Meanwhile, make the parsnip purée. Peel the parsnips and cut thick 'chips' from around the core. Discard the core. Chop the parsnips roughly. Heat the butter and olive oil in a shallow saucepan and gently sauté the parsnips and potato until pale golden brown. Pour in the stock, season and bring to the boil. Cover with one or two butter papers and simmer for about 15 minutes until the vegetables are soft and the liquid has evaporated.

5 Pour in the cream, bring back to the boil and simmer for a few minutes until almost all gone. Scoop into a food processor and whiz until very velvety and smooth. Check the seasoning.

6 Dish the oxtails on to warmed serving plates or a large serving platter. Strain the cooking liquid, reheat and nappé the oxtail. To garnish, I suggest diagonal slices of carrots cooked with a little butter, water and crushed garlic. Really nice. Serve with the parsnip purée.

Herb-crusted rack of lamb with tomato farci

Lamb is a popular dish on our restaurant menu at all times of the year, but particularly associated with spring. We like to serve lamb racks with a light herb crust, which is rolled out in a sheet and pressed on to the part-roasted meat. The bits of crust that fall off are mixed into a finely chopped ratatouille mixture and spooned high into plum tomato shells. Some baby new potatoes make the nicest accompaniment. **SERVES 4**

2 racks of new season's lamb,
  about 300g each, chined
4 large plum tomatoes
2 tablespoons olive oil
1 medium courgette, finely chopped
½ small red pepper, finely chopped
½ small yellow pepper, finely chopped
½ small aubergine, finely chopped
sea salt and freshly ground black pepper

Crust
200g unsweetened brioche crumbs
  or rich white breadcrumbs
1 tablespoon chopped fresh basil
1 tablespoon chopped fresh chives
1 teaspoon fresh thyme leaves
50g butter, softened

1 Trim the lamb racks. Remove the chine bone and long sinew. Score the fat with the tip of a sharp knife into neat diamonds.

2 Make the herb crust. Blitz the crumbs in a food processor with the herbs and seasoning, then add the butter. Whiz until the crumbly mixture can be pinched with your fingers to a paste – what the French call a *pommade*. Line a wooden board with cling film and tip the mixture on top. Cover with more cling film, and roll out with a rolling pin to a sheet approximately the same area as the fat area of the two lamb racks. Chill the crust in the cling film.

3 To prepare the tomatoes, dip briefly in boiling water and then skin. Cut off a quarter of each at the top and chop into fine dice. Scoop out the seeds from the tomato shells and discard.

4 Heat the oil in a pan and sauté the courgette, peppers and aubergine for about 5 minutes, until just softened. Season nicely, then bind together with the tomato dice and set aside.

5 Preheat the oven to 200°C, Gas 6. Heat a heavy non-stick frying pan and, when hot, brown the fat side of each lamb rack. Turn to brown as much of the meat as possible. Remove from the heat. Stand the racks upright and allow the juices to run down in the pan.

6 Cut the herb crust into two pieces the same size as the racks and press on to the hot fat surface firmly with your fingers. The *pommade* is made with less butter than normal, so it sticks better. Mix any crust trimmings into the vegetables. Set the lamb, crust side up, in a roasting tin and roast for 10–12 minutes until the meat feels lightly springy when pressed.

7 Meanwhile, fill the tomato shells with the vegetable and *pommade* mix, piling it up high. Place the tomatoes in a baking dish with a trickle of olive oil and roast in the oven with the meat until hot and the tops crisp a little.

8 Allow the lamb to rest for 5–10 minutes before cutting each rack in half or into individual cutlets. Serve with the tomatoes, and trickle over any *jus* from the roasting tin.

Rump of new season's lamb with lentils

This is a good homely dish similar to many served up and down France. We call this cut of lamb rump, but you will know it better as chump. We serve the lamb with creamy gratin potatoes. By par-cooking potatoes in milk before finishing them in ramekins, they cook more evenly. It's a neat little trick. **SERVES 4**

4 chumps of lamb, about 200g each

3–4 tablespoons olive oil

1 sprig fresh thyme

150g Puy lentils

1 medium carrot

½ small celeriac

1 medium leek

2 tablespoons coarsely chopped fresh parsley

4 tablespoons Vinaigrette (page 184)

sea salt and freshly ground black pepper

Gratin potatoes

400g medium, slightly waxy
  potatoes, such as Maris Piper

300ml milk

300ml double cream

1 clove garlic, sliced

1 sprig fresh thyme

1 bay leaf

75g Gruyère cheese, grated

1 Remove the central bone from the chumps. Trim off fat and neaten to nice rump shapes. Place in a bowl or food bag with half of the oil and the tips from the thyme sprig. Set aside to marinate in the fridge.

2 Cook the lentils in boiling salted water for about 15 minutes. Drain and season.

3 Cut the carrot, celeriac and leek into 1cm squares. Heat the remaining oil in a saucepan and sauté the vegetables until lightly browned, 5–7 minutes (we call this a *brunoise*). Mix with the lentils and half the parsley, then bind with 2 tablespoons of the vinaigrette. Set aside.

4 For the gratin potatoes, preheat the oven to 200°C, Gas 6. Peel the potatoes and slice thinly (use a mandolin or the slicing blade of a food processor). Bring the milk and cream to the boil with some sea salt, the garlic and herbs, and simmer for a couple of minutes. Add the sliced potatoes and simmer for about 5 minutes until just tender. Drain in a colander set over a bowl to catch the creamy milk.

5 Mix the potatoes gently with two-thirds of the cheese. Layer neatly into four medium ramekins or cocotte dishes, seasoning in between the layers. Spoon a little of the saved creamy milk on top of each ramekin and sprinkle with the last of the cheese. Place the ramekins on a baking sheet and bake for 8–10 minutes until the cheese just turns a golden brown.

6 Meanwhile, heat a heavy-based non-stick frying pan until really hot. Remove the lamb rumps from the bowl or food bag, wiping off any thyme tips, and brown for 3–5 minutes on each side, seasoning lightly as they cook. The lamb should be served lightly pink – medium rare.

7 Reheat the lentils and spoon into the centre of four plates. Place the rumps on top (slice them first, if you like). Deglaze the frying pan with the last of the vinaigrette, stirring for a minute, then spoon these juices over the lamb. Sprinkle with the remaining parsley. Serve the gratin potatoes, still in their individual dishes, on the same plate. Simple and delicious!

Loin of pork with choucroute and mustard cream sauce

Pork is at its best in the middle of winter. Do choose outdoor-reared pork, because it has so much more flavour than the alternative. Ask the butcher for a best end of the loin, with rind that has been well scored so it will crisp to light crackling. Talking of which, if you want nice crisp crackling, then follow my suggestion to sear the rind first in a hot pan before roasting.

With the pork, I like to serve choucroute cooked in the Alsace style with crispy lardons of bacon.

SERVES 4

1 boned pork loin joint, about 1kg
500g jar choucroute (sauerkraut)
2 tablespoons olive oil
1 onion, sliced
75g smoked lean bacon, cut in small cubes
800ml Dark chicken stock (page 184)
150ml double cream
1 tablespoon coarsegrain mustard
sea salt and freshly ground black pepper

1 Preheat the oven to 200°C, Gas 6. Heat a large frying pan on the hob until you can feel a strong heat rising. Put the joint of pork in the pan, rind down, and press on to the hot pan (you might want to wrap your hand in a cloth to protect it). This will start the crackling crisping. Turn the joint and brown the rest of it.

2 Transfer the joint to a roasting tin, placing it rind side up, and sprinkle with sea salt. Roast for 30 minutes, then turn the temperature down to 180°C, Gas 4. Roast for a further 30 minutes. Do not baste.

3 Meanwhile, rinse the choucroute in cold water and drain well. Heat 1 tablespoon of oil in a large saucepan and gently sauté the onion for 5 minutes until lightly coloured. Stir in the bacon and continue cooking for about 3 minutes until crisp. Mix in the choucroute, and stir in 500ml of the stock and freshly ground pepper. Bring to the boil, then cover and simmer very gently for about 20 minutes.

4 Meanwhile, boil the remaining stock until reduced by half. Tip out of the pan and save, and pour the cream into the pan. Bring the cream to the boil, slowly, then mix in the reduced stock plus the mustard. Check the seasoning and keep the sauce warm.

5 When the pork is nearing the end of its cooking, pierce the thickest section with a thin skewer. Clear juices should run out. If not, cook it for longer until the juices are clear. The pork should feel just firm when pressed, but not rock solid. Remove from the oven and allow to rest for about 10 minutes whilst you reheat the sauce and divide the choucroute among four warmed plates.

6 Carve the pork into fairly thick slices, and break up the crackling into pieces. Place on top of the choucroute, and nappé with the sauce. Sheer rustic pleasure.

Hot Puddings

Baked apples with peppercorns

For this recipe you need to use a variety of dessert apple that holds its shape and texture well on baking – such as Granny Smith or Braeburn. After the initial caramelising, the apples are flavoured with crushed peppercorns and vanilla and baked in the oven until tender. I find that peppercorns really enhance the flavour of sweet things – especially fruits. **SERVES 6**

6 firm dessert apples, such as Granny Smith
   or Braeburn
about 100g butter, softened until runny but
   not melted
about 100g unrefined demerara sugar
300ml apple juice
1 teaspoon crushed black peppercorns
1 teaspoon crushed dried pink peppercorns
1 vanilla pod, slit open
2–3 tablespoons Armagnac (optional)

1 Peel the apples neatly using a small paring knife, and scoop out the cores with an apple corer. Pat dry with kitchen paper towel, then brush all over with the softened butter. Roll in the demerara sugar to coat.

2 Preheat the oven to 190°C, Gas 5. Place the apples in a roasting tin or baking dish and roast in the oven for 10 minutes.

3 Pour in the apple juice and scatter over the crushed peppercorns and vanilla pod. Spoon the juice over the apples, then return to the oven. Roast, uncovered, for a further 20 minutes, basting the fruits every 5 minutes or so. On the final basting, trickle over the Armagnac, if using.

4 Allow to cool for 10 minutes or longer, basting the apples occasionally with the pan juices.

5 To serve, lift the apples into a serving dish and strain the pan juices over. Serve warm with pouring cream or Crème anglaise (page 185).

Slow roasted peaches with orange caramel sauce

Here you need to roast peaches whole and unskinned, basting them from time to time with an orange caramel sauce. The texture holds up nicely and the flavour is very good. For an extra special dessert, partner with White peach parfaits (page 163), as illustrated (on page 162).
SERVES 6

250g caster sugar

3 tablespoons water

250ml fresh orange juice

1 vanilla pod

6 medium white peaches

50g unsalted butter, softened until runny
  but not melted

To serve (optional)
Sugar-crusted basil leaves (page 163)

1 Put 150g of the caster sugar and the water in a heavy-based saucepan and dissolve over a low heat. When the sugar syrup is completely clear, increase the heat and cook to a light caramel, about 5 minutes.

2 Remove from the heat and carefully stir in the orange juice; it will splutter. Slit open the vanilla pod, scrape out the seeds and add these to the caramel sauce. Set aside to cool until thickened.

3 Preheat the oven to 150°C, Gas 2. Brush the peaches liberally with the butter using a pastry brush, then sprinkle with the remaining sugar and roll them to coat thoroughly.

4 Place the peaches in a small roasting tin and spoon the caramel over them. Roast, uncovered, in the oven for about 30 minutes until the peaches are softened but still whole, basting them with the pan juices every 10 minutes or so.

5 Cover loosely with a 'tent' of foil and leave to cool; this encourages juices to gather in the bottom of the tin.

6 Peel off the loose peach skins. Stir up the pan juices and strain through a sieve into a jug.

7 Serve the peaches lightly chilled, with the orange caramel sauce spooned over. I sometimes top the peaches with sugar-crusted basil leaves.

Roasted black figs with spiced balsamic syrup

Make this simple recipe when you find large black Mission figs in the shops during late summer. The aromatic syrup can be strained after baking and used again. **SERVES 6**

6 large black Mission figs

3 tablespoons Acacia or pine-scented
  clear honey

150ml Stock syrup (page 185)

2 cinnamon sticks

2 cloves

2 vanilla pods, slit open

3 star anise

strips of zest from 1 orange

3 tablespoons aged balsamic vinegar

1 Trim the tips off the fig stalks and stand the figs in a medium shallow roasting tin. Preheat the oven to 150°C, Gas 2.

2 Meanwhile, put all the remaining ingredients into a heavy-based saucepan, bring to the boil and boil until reduced to a syrupy glaze, about 3 minutes.

3 Spoon the syrup over the figs. Bake uncovered for about 30 minutes, basting every 10 minutes or so, until the figs are soft when pierced with a skewer but still holding their shape.

4 Serve the figs warm, with a little syrup spooned over. Strain the rest of the sauce into a screw-topped jar and refrigerate for another time.

Variation Use green figs and omit the cinnamon, cloves, star anise and balsamic vinegar for a more subtle honey-flavoured syrup.

Classic crêpes suzette

For this classic dessert, you simply flavour a basic crêpe batter with grated orange zest and bathe the cooked crêpes in a warm, tangy orange sauce spiked with Grand Marnier. This isn't a dessert for a large party – up to 4 servings is manageable. **SERVES 4**

Crêpe batter
125g plain flour
2 good pinches of salt
1 or 2 medium free-range eggs
1 tablespoon melted butter
300ml milk
sunflower oil, to grease the pan

Sauce
6 large oranges
50g demerara sugar
about 90–100ml Grand Marnier

To finish
knob of unsalted butter

1 To make the crêpe batter, put the flour and salt in a food processor and add the eggs, melted butter and half the milk. Whiz until smooth and creamy, scraping down the sides once or twice. With the motor running, mix in the remaining milk, then pour into a jug. Finely grate the zest from two of the oranges (for the sauce) and stir into the batter.

2 To make the sauce, finely pare the zest from a further 2 oranges, using a swivel vegetable peeler, and cut into fine julienne strips. Blanch these in boiling water for 1 minute, then drain and pat dry; set aside. Squeeze the juice from 3 oranges and strain to remove pips. Peel and segment the other 3 oranges, cutting away the peel and pith with a sharp knife, then cutting between the membranes to release the segments. Set aside.

3 Heat the sugar in a heavy-based saucepan over a low heat until melted; avoid stirring but shake the pan a little to encourage the process. Once every grain has dissolved, add the orange zest julienne and simmer for 2 minutes or until the syrup forms a light caramel. Don't let the sugar burn or the sauce will taste bitter.

4 When the sugar syrup starts to caramelise, carefully add the Grand Marnier – it will splutter – and cook for a minute or so to burn off the alcohol.

5 Pour in the orange juice and boil until reduced by half. Remove from the heat, slide in the orange segments and leave to cool and macerate until warm.

6 Meanwhile, cook the crêpes. Heat a 20–23cm heavy-based crêpe pan or frying pan (preferably non-stick) until you can feel a good heat rising. Add a few drops of oil, tilt to grease the base of the pan, then tip out any excess. Pour in about 2–3 tablespoons crêpe batter from a ladle. Immediately swirl the pan so the batter coats the entire base thinly. Cook until the batter is set and little holes appear in the surface, about 1½ minutes. Slip a palette knife under the crêpe, then flip it over. Cook the other side for about 30 seconds. Slide the crêpe out on to a clean tea towel. Keep wrapped while cooking the rest of the batter; you will need 8 or 12 crêpes in total.

7 When ready to serve, melt a little butter in a large frying pan and add a cooked crêpe. Reheat for a few seconds and fold into quarters. Repeat with another one or two crêpes (for one serving). Spoon over a portion of orange sauce, making sure you include some segments and zest julienne. Slide on to a warmed dessert plate. Repeat and repeat, allowing 2–3 crêpes per serving.

Cherry and almond clafoutis

This is based on the classic French favourite. Here an almond-flavoured batter is baked in a shallow pan over a layer of pitted fresh cherries. Prepare the batter and fruits in advance, but put them together and bake the pudding at the last minute. The batter benefits from resting for a full 24 hours. You can either make one large pudding or 6 small ones (see below). **SERVES 6**

50g ground almonds
15g strong plain flour
good pinch of sea salt
100g caster sugar
2 large free-range eggs
3 large free-range egg yolks
250ml double cream
300g ripe fresh cherries
unsalted butter, softened, to grease pan
icing sugar, sifted, for dusting

1 Put the ground almonds, flour, salt and sugar into a food processor and whiz for a few seconds to combine. Add the eggs, egg yolks and cream and blend to a smooth batter, scraping down the sides of the bowl once or twice. Tip into a jug or bowl, cover and refrigerate for 24 hours.

2 In the meantime, remove the stones from the cherries and pat them dry if they are particularly juicy. Rub the inside of a large ovenproof sauté pan or gratin dish, about 23–25cm in diameter, with softened butter.

3 Preheat the oven to 190°C, Gas 5. Scatter the cherries over the base of the pan or dish. Stir the batter in the jug, then pour over the cherries. Bake for about 20 minutes until risen and golden brown. The middle may be slightly flatter than the surrounding batter but it should be set. If not, then bake for a little longer.

4 Dust with icing sugar and serve at once.

To make individual clafoutis Butter six 10cm tartlet tins or Yorkshire pudding tins and divide the cherries between them. Pour on the batter and bake at 200°C, Gas 6 for about 12 minutes.

Orange curd layer pudding

This delightful old-fashioned pudding cooks to a delicious light soufflé sponge on top, with a thick zingy curd sauce underneath. It looks like a nightmare just before you bake it, all runny and slightly lumpy – the transformation is little short of a miracle. I wonder whoever first thought of such a recipe, or was it a happy accident? Bake it in a heatproof glass dish to reveal the appealing layers – I use a Bodum glass soufflé dish. For a dinner party, add a splash of Grand Marnier or Cointreau. **SERVES 4–6**

300ml fresh orange juice
grated zest and juice of 1 lemon
3 tablespoons Grand Marnier or Cointreau
  (optional)
60g butter, softened, plus extra to grease dish
100g caster sugar
4 large free-range eggs, separated
60g self-raising flour
½ teaspoon baking powder
150ml milk
icing sugar, for dusting

1 Put the orange and lemon juices in a saucepan, bring to the boil and boil until reduced by just over half – to 150ml. Set aside to cool and then stir in the liqueur, if using.
2 Butter the sides of a 1 litre soufflé dish, or other similar ovenproof dish. Preheat the oven to 180°C, Gas 4.
3 In a mixing bowl, beat the butter with the caster sugar and lemon zest until soft and creamy. Beat in the egg yolks, one at a time. Sift the flour and baking powder together over the mixture, then beat in.
4 Slowly add the citrus juice and milk to the mixture, stirring to blend. Do not worry if the mixture looks curdled or lumpy at this stage. It will be fine. Trust me – I'm a chef.
5 Now whisk the egg whites in another bowl until they form softly stiff peaks. Beat a third of the whisked egg whites into the cake mixture, then carefully fold in the rest using a large metal spoon and a figure-of-eight motion.
6 Stand the prepared dish in a roasting tin, then pour in the mixture. Surround the dish with boiling water to create a bain-marie and place in the oven. Bake for 1–1¼ hours until the pudding is golden brown and firm on top, and creamy underneath. Reduce the oven temperature slightly towards the end of cooking if the top appears to be browning too quickly.
7 Remove the dish from the bain-marie and leave to stand for 10 minutes or a little longer. Dust the pudding with icing sugar before serving. As you spoon it out, make sure you get right down to the bottom to include some of the soft curd layer. There's no need for pouring cream, unless you really must.

Baguette and butter pudding laced with Baileys

Most chefs now seem to have their own version of bread and butter pudding, using rich breads such as panettone, pain au chocolat and brioche. I like to use thin slices of French bread or croissants – these allow the richness of the eggy custard to come through. A good splash of Baileys cream liqueur takes this into the ethereal. Serve the pudding warm, not piping hot, trickled with a little more Baileys if you like. SERVES 6

50g butter, softened
½ large French stick (about 150g), thinly sliced
60g sultanas or dried cranberries, or a mixture
   of both
2 large free-range eggs
2 large free-range egg yolks
40g caster sugar
300ml double cream
300ml milk
4 tablespoons Baileys cream liqueur, or more
   to taste
demerara sugar, for sprinkling
3 tablespoons apricot jam

1 Use a large knob of the butter to grease the sides of a 1.5 litre shallow ovenproof dish. Spread the bread slices with the remaining butter. Arrange the bread in the dish in overlapping layers, sprinkling the dried fruit in between.

2 Beat the whole eggs, egg yolks and sugar together in a large bowl until creamy, then beat in the cream, milk and Baileys. Slowly pour this mixture over the bread. Press the bread slices down gently with your fingers so they are completely submerged.

3 Leave to stand for about 20 minutes to allow the bread to soak up the custard. Preheat the oven to 180°C, Gas 4.

4 Stand the dish in a roasting tin and surround with boiling water to come halfway up the sides of the dish. (A bain-marie is used to avoid overheating the custard, which otherwise might curdle.) Sprinkle with demerara sugar and bake for 40–50 minutes until golden. Shortly before this time is up, warm the apricot jam until runny.

5 Dab the apricot glaze over the surface of the pudding and leave to stand for 15 minutes before serving. The custard will continue to cook and firm up during this time. Trickle a little more Baileys over each portion to serve if you like.

Thai rice pudding with coconut and lemon grass

Possibly the fastest rice pudding in the West. I use delicate, fragrant, slightly sticky Thai jasmine rice and cook it in salted water in the traditional Thai way, adding sugar and coconut cream afterwards. To enrich it further, I suggest you stir in a little double cream. Serve this pudding warm and creamy, with a tangy mango accompaniment. **SERVES 4**

250g Thai jasmine rice
1 fresh lemon grass stalk, slit almost in half
500ml water
½ teaspoon fine sea salt
100g caster sugar
200ml carton coconut cream
4 tablespoons double cream, plus extra to
  serve (optional)
mango slices, to serve

1 Put the rice, lemon grass, water and salt into a medium heavy-based saucepan. Bring to the boil, stirring once or twice, then turn the heat to low, cover and simmer for 12 minutes.
2 Remove the pan from the heat and, without removing the lid, leave to stand for 5 minutes.
3 Remove the lemon grass. Add the sugar and stir until dissolved, then stir in the coconut cream. Leave to stand, covered, for a further 5 minutes. Add the double cream.
4 Serve the rice pudding warm rather than hot, adding a little extra cream if you like. Top each serving with a fan of mango slices.

Variation This is also delicious served cold, as a condé. Leave the rice pudding to cool completely, then stir in some single cream to loosen it. Put a layer of sliced mango, apricots or peaches in the base of 6 sundae dishes and spoon over the rice. Chill lightly before serving, sprinkled with chopped roasted pistachios or almonds.

Little white chocolate and kahlua soufflés

These individual soufflés look very appealing with their cocoa-dusted tops. Effectively they are based on a white chocolate crème pâtissière. I like to bake the mixture over a layer of marinated cherries and serve the soufflés with a warm plum coulis (see below). You simply spoon the coulis into the centre of the hot soufflés as you serve them. **SERVES 6**

150g white chocolate

250ml milk

10g cornflour

15g plain flour

3 large free-range eggs, separated

75g caster sugar

100ml Kahlua or Tia Maria liqueur

40g unsalted butter, very soft

4–6 tablespoons grated dark chocolate, or ground almonds or hazelnuts

6 tablespoons bottled dark red cherries, drained and pitted (optional)

4 tablespoons double cream

cocoa powder, for dusting

1 Break up the white chocolate and place in a large bowl. Heat the milk in a heavy-based saucepan until boiling, then slowly pour on to the chocolate, stirring until melted.

2 Sift the cornflour and flour together. Beat the egg yolks and 50g of the sugar together in a bowl, then mix in the flours, beating until smooth.

3 Slowly pour on the hot chocolate milk, stirring briskly. Return to the saucepan and stir over a gentle heat until thickened and smooth. Simmer gently, stirring, for about 30 seconds, then remove from the heat.

4 Meanwhile, boil the coffee liqueur in a small pan until reduced by about half. Stir into the chocolate crème pâtissière. Set aside to cool.

5 Using a pastry brush, coat the insides of six individual 150ml (¼ pint) soufflé dishes with soft butter using vertical strokes, then chill until set. Brush with a second layer of butter, then tip the grated chocolate or ground nuts into the dishes and rotate to ensure the sides and base are evenly and liberally coated. If using cherries, divide them between the dishes. Preheat the oven to 190°C, Gas 5.

6 Beat the cream into the chilled chocolate mixture to loosen it a little. Whisk the egg whites in a clean bowl until they stand in peaks, then gradually whisk in the remaining 25g sugar. Fold this meringue into the chocolate crème pâtissière.

7 Divide the mixture between the prepared dishes and level the tops with a palette knife or back of a spoon. Place on a baking tray and bake for 15–18 minutes until risen and golden brown. Dust the tops with cocoa as you take the soufflés from the oven and serve instantly.

Plum coulis Stone 200g ripe plums and purée in a blender or food processor with 4 tablespoons Stock syrup (page 185) until smooth. Add a tablespoon of brandy or kirsch to enhance the flavour. Rub through a sieve and warm through gently in a small pan.

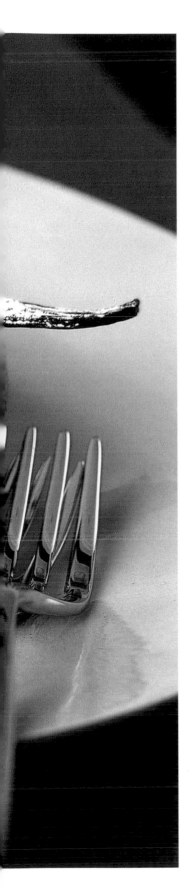

Caramelised apple tart

Making a fruit tart with crisp pastry and tender fruit can be tricky. The answer is to bake it upside down, so the fruit juices do not leach into the pastry and make it soggy. Ideally, make this tart in a shallow metal pan that will go into the oven, such as a gratin pan, paella pan or proper tarte Tatin tin (in the restaurant, we make individual tarts and decorate with a slit vanilla pod dusted with icing sugar). Serve with scoops of Classic vanilla ice cream (page 158), or quenelles of mascarpone or clotted cream. **SERVES 2–3**

3 large Cox's apples
300g Puff pastry (page 185)
40g cold unsalted butter, thinly sliced
80g caster sugar mixed with
   ¼ teaspoon Chinese five-spice powder

1 About 4 hours before cooking, quarter the apples, cut out the core and peel thinly. Leave the apple quarters uncovered so they oxidise a little and dry out. It doesn't matter if they brown because, of course, they will be coated in a caramel anyway.
2 Roll out the pastry and cut out a circle 23–24cm in diameter (this is assuming you will be making a tart of 20–21cm diameter). You may find it helpful to use a large round cake tin as a template. Prick lightly with the tip of a sharp knife and chill for an hour or two.
3 Preheat the oven to 200°C, Gas 6. When ready to cook, layer the thinly sliced hard butter in the bottom of your pan and sprinkle over the spiced sugar. Press the apple quarters into the butter, cored side uppermost, arranging them in a circle with one in the centre.
4 Place the pan over a medium heat. After a few minutes, start to roll the pan so the butter and sugar dissolve and mix together. Tip the pan occasionally so you can check that the caramel is forming. Cook like this for a total of 10 minutes, then remove from the heat.
5 Lay the pastry over the pan and tuck the edges down inside, pressing in with a fork. Place the pan in the oven (take care because the caramel will be hot). Bake for about 15 minutes until the pastry is golden brown and crisp. Remove and cool before up-ending on to a large round platter. If the caramel sticks fast, then reheat it for a few minutes to melt.

Roasted rhubarb and apple crumble

Crumbles can be heavy, stodgy puddings. This is an altogether lighter affair, made in an ovenproof sauté pan. The filling is caramelised yet sharp and fruity, and the fudgey topping is scattered on loosely so it bakes to a crisp crunch. Many other fruits and spices complement rhubarb, including apple, vanilla and nutmeg. Serve the crumble warm, with pouring cream or Crème anglaise (page 185). **SERVES 4**

500g pink tender rhubarb
1 large Braeburn apple
100g vanilla sugar (see below)

Topping
100g plain flour
50g butter, chilled and cut into small cubes
50g light muscovado sugar
freshly grated nutmeg, to taste
40g porridge oats

1 Preheat the oven to 190°C, Gas 5. Trim off the ends of the rhubarb, then cut into chunks about 5cm long. Wash if necessary and pat dry in a clean tea towel. Quarter, core and thinly peel the apple. Cut into chunks, about 2cm in size.
2 Heat an enamelled cast-iron or other heavy-based sauté pan until very hot; it should almost start to smoke.
3 Toss the rhubarb and apple in the vanilla sugar, then tip into the pan and spread out to a single layer. The fruit will start to caramelise almost immediately if the pan is at the right temperature. Leave for a couple of minutes, then turn with a thin metal spoon or spatula so the fruit stays intact as far as possible; it shouldn't become too mushy.
4 Continue cooking for a further 3–5 minutes until the rhubarb and apple pieces feel just tender when pierced with the tip of a knife. Remove from the heat and leave to cool slightly while you make the topping.
5 Put the flour and butter in a food processor and process briefly until the mixture resembles fine crumbs. Add the muscovado sugar and whiz for a few seconds more. Grate the nutmeg straight into the mixture, add the oats and blend again briefly.
6 Scatter the topping over the fruit – don't pat it down or level it. Bake the pudding for 20 minutes until the topping is nicely browned. Leave to stand for 10 minutes before serving.

Vanilla sugar Simply bury 3 vanilla pods in a jar containing about 500g caster sugar. Within a couple of days you will have fragrant vanilla sugar. We find this a good use for split pods that have had their seeds extracted – they still impart lots of flavour.

Steamed chocolate pudding

This scrumptious rich pudding is for all chocoholics. It is simple to make – the only tricky part is remembering to top up the pan with boiling water during steaming. I like to serve the pudding with a white chocolate sauce, but you could serve it with Crème anglaise (page 185) or pouring cream. **SERVES 4–6**

125g caster or soft brown sugar
125g butter, softened
3 medium free-range eggs
2 tablespoons coffee essence
100g self-raising flour
25g cocoa powder
¼ teaspoon fine sea salt
½ teaspoon baking powder
75g fresh white breadcrumbs

Topping
50g muscovado sugar
50g butter, softened

White chocolate sauce
100g white chocolate
150ml double cream

1 Lightly grease a 1 litre heatproof pudding basin. For the topping, mix together the 50g muscovado sugar and butter in the prepared basin, then spread the mixture over the base and a third of the way up the sides.

2 Whiz the pudding ingredients, except the breadcrumbs, in a food processor or mixer until smooth. Add the breadcrumbs and pulse lightly until just incorporated.

3 Spoon the mixture into the pudding basin. Cover with greaseproof paper and foil, pleated together in the centre (to allow room for the pudding to rise), and secure under the rim with kitchen string.

4 Steam the pudding for 2 hours, using a steamer or large saucepan containing enough boiling water to come halfway up the sides of the basin. Check the water level periodically and top up with boiling water as necessary. Leave the pudding to stand for 10 minutes.

5 Meanwhile, make the sauce. Break the chocolate into pieces and place in a heatproof bowl. Pour over the cream. Place the bowl over a saucepan of gently simmering water until the chocolate has melted. Stir to blend the chocolate with the cream. Cool until tepid.

6 Remove the cover and run a table knife around the side of the pudding. Turn the pudding out on to a warmed plate and serve with the white chocolate sauce.

Steamed toffee, banana and pecan pudding

To my mind this is the ultimate comfort pudding and it is so easy to whiz up in a mixer. For a light texture, I use half breadcrumbs and half flour. **SERVES 4–6**

1 large ripe banana

3 ripe passion fruit, or 1 unwaxed lemon

125g butter, softened

125g caster sugar

3 medium free-range eggs

100g self-raising flour

¼ teaspoon fine sea salt

½ teaspoon baking powder

75g fresh white breadcrumbs

Topping

50g butter, softened

50g light muscovado sugar

50g pecan halves

Toffee sauce

300ml double cream

170g light muscovado sugar

4 tablespoons liquid glucose

70g unsalted butter

1 Lightly grease a 1 litre heatproof pudding basin. To make the topping, cream the 50g butter and muscovado sugar together in the basin until nicely blended, then spread it around the base and a third of the way up the sides. Press 6 pecan halves down into the topping in a circle. Chop the rest of the nuts and reserve.

2 To make the pudding, mash the banana to a pulp. If using passion fruit, halve and scrape out the pulp into a sieve over a bowl. Rub through to extract the juice; discard the seeds. If using lemon, grate the zest and squeeze the juice.

3 Put the butter, caster sugar, eggs, flour, salt, baking powder and passion fruit juice (or lemon juice and zest) in a food processor or mixer. Whiz until smooth and creamy, scraping down the sides once or twice. Add the banana pulp, chopped pecans and breadcrumbs and pulse lightly until just incorporated.

4 Spoon the mixture into the pudding basin. For the cover, lay a large piece of greaseproof paper on a sheet of foil and pleat them together in the centre (to allow for the pudding to rise). Place over the basin and secure tightly under the rim with kitchen string.

5 Place in a steamer over boiling water, or in a large saucepan containing enough boiling water to come halfway up the sides of the basin. Steam for 2 hours, checking the water level every 30 minutes or so and topping up with boiling water as necessary.

6 Meanwhile, make the sauce. Put half the cream in a heavy-based saucepan with the sugar, glucose and butter. Heat slowly, stirring, until the sugar is dissolved, then raise the heat and boil for about 10 minutes, to a light toffee colour, stirring once or twice so it doesn't burn on the base. Immediately remove from the heat and allow to cool, stirring occasionally to prevent a skin forming. When the sauce is cold, beat in the remaining cream.

7 Lift the basin out of the pan and let the pudding stand for 10 minutes. Uncover and run a knife around the side of the pudding. Unmould on to a warm plate and serve, with the toffee sauce.

Ices and
Cool Desserts

Espresso coffee granita

This is the ultimate iced coffee. First you need to make some very strong coffee, then blend it with stock syrup in the proportion of 2 to 1. If you have a home espresso machine, this recipe is particularly appropriate. The finer the flavour of the coffee the better the granita. I infuse it with cardamom and orange zest to give it an Arabian slant, but you can omit these if you prefer.
SERVES 6–8

100g sugar
150ml water
2 cardamom pods
1 or 2 strips of orange zest
500ml strong fresh coffee, cooled

1 Put the sugar and water in a saucepan over a low heat, stirring occasionally, until dissolved. Add the cardamom pods and orange zest and boil for 3 minutes. Remove from the heat, cool for 1 hour and then discard the cardamom pods and orange zest.
2 Mix the coffee with the infused syrup and chill.
3 Transfer to a shallow rigid container and freeze for 2–3 hours until partially frozen. Take the semi-frozen granita from the freezer and stir the frozen crystals into the liquid, using a fork; return to the freezer. Beat lightly twice more during freezing to achieve a granular texture.
4 To serve, scrape shavings off the frozen block of granita with a strong spoon. Serve at once in elegant wine glasses or sundae dishes.

Variation

LEMON GRASS GRANITA This truly refreshing water ice has a subtle fragrance and a hint of tropical flavour. Heat 500ml water, 125g caster sugar and 3 tablespoons liquid glucose slowly in a heavy-based saucepan, stirring occasionally, until the sugar has dissolved. Increase the heat and boil the syrup for about 3 minutes. Take off the heat and stir in the grated zest of 1 lime or small lemon, the juice of 1 lemon, 4 chopped lemon grass stalks and a sprig of lemon balm (if available). Set aside to infuse until cold. Strain the infused syrup into a shallow freezer container and freeze until almost solid, beating lightly with a fork two or three times as it freezes. Serve as above.

Classic vanilla ice cream

You can always tell a real vanilla ice cream – it will be pale yellow and speckled with tiny black vanilla seeds. Crème Anglaise is the basis of this delicious ice cream. SERVES 8–10

500ml whole milk
500ml double cream
100g caster sugar
12 large free-range egg yolks
2–3 vanilla pods, split

1 Put the milk and cream in a heavy-based saucepan with 1 tablespoon of the sugar. Scrape out the seeds from the vanilla pods and add them to the pan, together with the empty pods. Slowly bring to the boil, then remove from the heat and leave to infuse for 10 minutes. Meanwhile, using a balloon whisk, beat the egg yolks and remaining sugar together in a large bowl set on a damp cloth (to hold it steady) until pale golden and creamy. Remove the vanilla pods from the infused milk, then bring back to the boil. Pour a third of the liquid on to the egg mixture, whisking well. Gradually pour in the rest of the milk mixture, whisking continuously.
2 Return to the pan and cook over a very low heat, stirring continuously with a wooden spoon until it thickens slightly – enough to coat the back of the spoon thinly. Immediately strain into a chilled bowl. Cool quickly over a bowl of iced water, then cover and chill thoroughly.
3 Pour the chilled crème anglaise into an ice cream machine and churn. When the ice cream is almost firm, you can transfer it to a freezer container, seal and put into the freezer unless, of course, you are serving it at once. If you don't have an ice cream machine, freeze the mixture in a shallow container, beating two or three times during freezing to break down the ice crystals.
4 For optimum flavour, eat within 1 week, softening the ice cream at room temperature for about 10 minutes before serving.

Variations

CARDAMOM ICE CREAM Make as above, omitting the vanilla. Instead, steep 1 tablespoon green cardamom pods in the creamy milk. Strain the crème anglaise after, rather than before chilling.

GINGER ICE CREAM Make as above, omitting the vanilla from the crème anglaise. Instead, peel and grate a 3cm cube of fresh root ginger and steep in the creamy milk. For extra flavour, stir 2 finely chopped pieces of preserved stem ginger (drained of syrup) into the cooled custard.

STRAWBERRY ICE CREAM Make half the above quantity of crème anglaise and chill. Purée 500g ripe strawberries in a food processor or blender. Transfer to a deep heavy-based pan and boil to reduce by half. This takes 10–15 minutes and concentrates the flavour. Cool. Strain to remove the seeds. Beat the strawberry purée into the chilled crème anglaise and continue as above.

CHOCOLATE CHIP ICE CREAM Churn a quantity of Classic vanilla ice cream until slushy. Finely chop 150g dark chocolate, add to the ice cream and continue churning until firm.

Raspberry sorbet

This is a beautiful purple-red sorbet that I could just eat and eat. You do need to use fresh home-grown raspberries in season and naturally I prefer Scottish ones – they're the best. The syrup is strong to accentuate the flavour of the fruit. **SERVES 6–8**

700g raspberries
juice of 1 small lemon
300ml water
200g caster sugar
3 tablespoons liquid glucose

1 Put the raspberries in a food processor or blender with the lemon juice. Whiz to a smooth purée then transfer to a bowl, cover and chill.

2 Meanwhile, put the water and sugar in a heavy-based pan and dissolve over a low heat. When the syrup is clear, increase the heat to medium and boil for 5 minutes. Stir in the glucose and cool.

3 Mix the cooled sugar syrup with the raspberry purée. Pass through a sieve into a bowl to remove the seeds, rubbing the mixture through with the back of the ladle.

4 Churn in an ice cream machine until almost frozen solid, then transfer to a rigid plastic container and put in the freezer. Alternatively, freeze in a shallow container, beating two or three times during freezing. Serve in scoops or shavings.

Variations

DARK BERRY SORBET Make as above, replacing the raspberries with 500g fresh blackcurrants, 125g blackberries and 125g blueberries; increase the sugar to 250g; reduce the water to 200ml. Put the blackcurrants in a heavy-based saucepan and heat gently until the skins burst. Continue to simmer for a further 2–3 minutes, then take off the heat and set aside to cool. Put the cooled blackcurrants in a food processor or blender with the other fruit and the lemon juice and whiz to a purée. Transfer to a bowl, cover and chill, then continue as above.

STRAWBERRY SORBET Make as above, replacing the raspberries with strawberries and using the juice of 2 small lemons. Put the strawberries and lemon juice in a food processor or blender and whiz to a purée. Tip into a saucepan, bring to the boil and continue to boil until reduced by half. Transfer to a bowl, cover and chill, then continue as above.

Strawberry and vanilla semi-freddo

Parfaits are the ultimate make-ahead iced dessert – perfect for entertaining. They can be frozen well in advance – in individual or large moulds – and served within minutes of taking from the freezer. This is a very simple parfait – fresh fruit purée mixed with pâte à bombe and whipped cream. Make it when home-grown strawberries are at their peak – full of flavour and colour, vital qualities for frozen desserts. Ideally, serve the parfait sliced with some wild strawberries or assorted summer berries and trickles of fruit coulis. **SERVES 6–8**

250g strawberries, hulled
125g redcurrants, stripped from their
   stalks
150g caster sugar
100ml water
5 large free-range egg yolks
200ml double cream
1 vanilla pod

1 Purée the strawberries and redcurrants in a food processor or blender until smooth, then sieve to remove the seeds if preferred.
2 Put the sugar and water in a small heavy-based saucepan and heat slowly until completely dissolved and clear, stirring once or twice. Meanwhile, whisk the egg yolks in a heatproof bowl using a hand-held electric mixer on full speed until pale yellow, thick and creamy. Increase the heat under the pan of sugar syrup and boil until it registers 120°C on a sugar thermometer; ie the 'hard ball stage', when a little of the hot syrup dropped into a glass of cold water forms a firm, clear ball. This should take 5–7 minutes. As soon as the syrup reaches this stage, remove from the heat.
3 With the electric beaters still whirring, trickle the just-boiled syrup on to the whisked egg yolks. Carry on whisking with the mixer on full speed so the mixture increases in volume and becomes thick, foamy and creamy. Fold the fruit purée into the whisked mixture, then cover and chill for 1 hour.
4 Pour the cream into a bowl. Slit open the vanilla pod and scrape out the seeds with the tip of a knife, adding these to the cream. Three-quarters whip the cream until softly peaking. Fold the vanilla cream into the strawberry mixture, then freeze in a 1.2 litre loaf tin or individual moulds.
5 To unmould a large parfait, dip the mould into warm water for a few seconds, then invert on to a board and soften at room temperature for 5–10 minutes before slicing. Turn out individual parfaits straight on to serving plates.

White peach parfaits

Make this refreshing parfait at the height of summer when my favourite white peaches are in season. At other times, use other full flavoured juicy peaches or nectarines. For a special dessert, serve with Slow roasted peaches with orange caramel sauce (page 136). **SERVES 8–10**

500ml Stock syrup (page 185)
6 large basil leaves
150g caster sugar
100ml water
5 large free-range egg yolks
4 large white peaches
1 tablespoon crème de pêche
2 medium free-range egg whites

squeeze of lemon juice
100g caster sugar
150ml double cream

To serve (optional)
Sugar-crusted basil leaves (see below)
Oven-dried peach slices (page 186)

1 Prepare the stock syrup and add the basil leaves while it is hot; leave to steep as the syrup cools for about 30 minutes.

2 Meanwhile, put the sugar and water in a small heavy-based saucepan and heat slowly until completely dissolved and clear, stirring once or twice. Meanwhile, whisk the egg yolks in a heatproof bowl using a hand-held electric mixer on full speed until pale yellow, thick and creamy. Increase the heat under the pan of sugar syrup and boil until it registers 120°C on a sugar thermometer; ie the 'hard ball stage', when a little of the hot syrup dropped into a glass of cold water forms a firm, clear ball. This should take 5–7 minutes. As soon as the syrup reaches this stage, remove from the heat.

3 With the electric beaters still whirring, trickle the just-boiled syrup on to the whisked egg yolks. Carry on whisking with the mixer on full speed so the mixture increases in volume and becomes thick, foamy and creamy. Set aside.

4 To skin the peaches: immerse them in boiling water for 30 seconds, then into ice-cold water. Lift out and peel, then halve and stone. Strain the infused syrup into a medium pan. Add the peach halves and poach gently for 10 minutes, then drain (the syrup can be used again). Purée the peaches in a blender or food processor, turn into a bowl and mix in the crème de pêche.

5 In another bowl, whisk the egg whites with the lemon juice until softly stiff, then gradually whisk in the sugar to make a firm, glossy meringue.

6 Whip the cream until it just holds its shape, then fold into the peach purée with the meringue. Spoon into a 1.2 litre mould or 8–10 individual moulds, such as darioles. Freeze until solid.

7 To serve, unmould a large parfait by dipping the mould into warm water for a few seconds, then turn out on to a board and allow to soften for 5–10 minutes before slicing. Unmould individual parfaits straight on to serving plates. Surround with oven-dried peach slices and top with sugar-crusted basil leaves if you like.

Sugar-crusted leaves Dip small basil, mint or coriander leaves in lightly beaten egg white, then dust liberally with caster sugar. Place on a tray lined with baking parchment and leave to dry overnight in a warm dry spot, such as an airing cupboard.

Apricot compote with lemon and lime cream

A compote is a simple, thick purée of cooked or raw fruit, which we use as a base for fruit tarts, spoon into hot soufflés, or serve topped with a flavoured cream in shot glasses or other small glasses. For optimum flavour, use slightly over-ripe fruit, as the natural fruit sugars will be at their best and your compote will need little, if any extra sugar. This apricot compote is subtly flavoured with star anise and served topped with a citrus-flavoured cream. Confit of lemon and lime zest provides the finishing touch. Tell your guests to push their spoon right to the base of the glass – to savour all three layers at once. **SERVES 8–10**

500g ripe apricots
25g butter
2 tablespoons caster sugar
2 star anise

Lemon and lime cream
finely grated zest and juice of 2 large lemons
finely grated zest and juice of 3 limes
40g caster sugar
125g mascarpone
150ml double cream

To serve (optional)
Confit of lemon and lime zest (page 186)

1 Halve and stone the apricots, then cut into quarters. Melt the butter with the sugar in a heavy-based saucepan over a low heat and cook until it turns a light caramel colour.
2 Add the apricots and star anise. Cover the surface with a scrunched-up sheet of wet greaseproof paper. (This will allow some of the steam to escape, so the fruit is sautéed rather than stewed.) Cook on a medium heat for 10–15 minutes until very soft. Discard the star anise.
3 Now, off the heat, take a Bamix or stick blender to the pan and whiz the fruit to a purée. (Or purée in a food processor or blender.) Cool and chill until ready to use.
4 To make the lemon and lime cream, mix the grated zests and sugar together in a bowl. Bring the citrus juices to the boil in a small pan and boil until reduced to about 2 tablespoons. Pour on to the zesty sugar, stir and allow to cool.
5 Beat the cooled citrus sugar mixture into the mascarpone. Whip the cream until it forms soft floppy peaks and fold into the fruity mascarpone. Cover and chill lightly.
6 To serve, spoon the compote into small glasses and top with a spoonful of lemon and lime cream. Sprinkle with confit of lemon and lime zest if you like, then serve.

Minted melon salad

A selection of melons, scooped into balls and enhanced with a clove and mint flavoured syrup, makes a wonderfully refreshing dessert for a hot summer's day – especially if you serve it topped with shavings of Lemon grass granita (page 156), as illustrated. The different melons give a subtle variation in flavour, sweetness and colour. Checking the fruit for ripeness requires sniffing and gentle thumb pressure applied at the stalk end. We buy melons a few days ahead when they are fragrant but still quite firm, and let them ripen alongside a bunch of bananas.
SERVES 4–6

200ml light Stock syrup (page 185)
2 cloves
1 small Ogen or ½ honeydew melon
1 small Charentais melon
1 wedge of watermelon, about 400g
about 6–8 large mint leaves

1 Heat the stock syrup in a pan until almost boiling, then add the cloves, remove from the heat and set aside to infuse until cool.
2 Prepare the melons. Halve the whole fruit and deseed all the melons. Scoop the flesh into balls using a melon baller and place in a bowl. Pour over the cooled syrup and leave to macerate for 10 minutes. Discard the cloves.
3 Finely shred the mint leaves and gently stir into the melon salad. Leave to stand for a further 5 minutes, then serve.

Bananas in caramel rum syrup

Here bananas are steeped in a rich syrup with a hint of vanilla and spices. For a lively kick, I suggest adding white rum or my favourite treat, Malibu – then close your eyes and imagine a tropical beach. Choose bananas that are firm and only just ripe. **SERVES 4**

150g caster sugar
230ml water
juice of 1 lemon
2–3 tablespoons white rum or Malibu
1 vanilla pod
1 cinnamon stick
2 star anise
4 large, just ripe bananas

To serve (optional)
Flavoured crème fraîche (see below)

1 Put the sugar and 2 tablespoons of the water in a large shallow pan over a gentle heat, stirring once or twice until dissolved. When the sugar syrup is clear, raise the heat and cook to a light caramel, about 5 minutes.
2 Immediately remove from the heat, cool for 2 minutes then stir in the lemon juice, taking care as it will spit a little. Mix in the rum or Malibu and remaining 200ml water. Slit the vanilla pod lengthways and add to the syrup with the whole spices.
3 Peel the bananas and halve lengthways. Place in a single layer in the pan and spoon the caramel syrup over to coat them all over; this also prevents the bananas from discolouring.
4 Leave to macerate for 40 minutes before serving. A flavoured crème fraîche, such as lemon grass or ginger, is a nice complement.

Flavoured crème fraîche Full-fat crème fraîche can be whipped and flavoured with Stock syrup (page 185) which has been infused with vanilla, lemon grass or spices, allowing 2 tablespoons for every 200ml cream. Or try whipping crème fraîche with 2 tablespoons of the syrup from a jar of stem ginger for a simple ginger flavoured crème fraîche.

Espresso coffee crème brûlée

Crème brûlée comes in a variety of flavours. In the restaurant we serve basil, rosemary and lavender infused pots. For this coffee-flavoured cream you need to use a set of ovenproof coffee cups – such as the espresso set in the photograph. Chocolate-coated coffee beans add a chic finishing touch. **SERVES 6**

350ml double cream
125ml whole milk (preferably UHT)
50ml double strength espresso coffee
1 tablespoon Kahlua or Tia Maria (optional)
6 large free-range egg yolks
75g caster sugar

To serve
2 tablespoons demerara sugar, for caramelising
chocolate-coated coffee beans (optional)

1 Preheat the oven to 140°C, Gas 1. Lightly grease 6 ovenproof coffee cups and stand them on a baking tray.

2 Put the cream and milk in a heavy-based saucepan and heat slowly to scalding point, then stir in the espresso coffee and liqueur, if using.

3 Beat the egg yolks in a large heatproof bowl until pale and creamy. Pour the hot steaming coffee cream on to the egg yolks, a third at a time, whisking well. Then whisk in the caster sugar. Strain this liquid through a fine-mesh sieve into a jug.

4 Pour the mixture into the coffee cups, dividing it equally. Bake for about 45 minutes until the custards are very lightly set on top. To test, tilt one of the cups slightly: the custard should come away from the side of the cup and the centre should still be slightly wobbly. Remove from the oven and allow to cool; the mixture will thicken on cooling. Chill until required.

5 When ready to serve, sprinkle a teaspoon of demerara sugar evenly over the surface of each custard and caramelise with a blow-torch. Serve as soon as possible, with a few chocolate coffee beans if you like.

Note If you do not have a blow-torch, it is possible to caramelise the topping by placing the cups under a very hot grill. However, this is only effective if the grill is very hot, otherwise the set custard underneath can melt. If in doubt about your grill or the capacity of the cups to withstand grilling, omit the topping.

Mango and dark chocolate mousse

The unlikely combination of flavours in this recipe comes together beautifully. Why not serve it topped with Caramelised mango slices (page 186) as a special party mousse? **SERVES 6**

Pâte à bombe
150g caster sugar
100ml water
5 large free-range egg yolks

Italian meringue
120g caster sugar
1 teaspoon liquid glucose
2 tablespoons water
2 large free-range egg whites

To assemble
2 fresh apricots, halved, stoned and
 quartered, or 4 mi-cuit (no-need-to-
 soak) dried apricots
1 large, ripe (but not soft) mango,
 peeled, stoned and roughly chopped
1 tablespoon chopped fresh mint
200g dark chocolate (at least 60%
 cocoa solids)
300ml double cream

1 To make the pâte à bombe, put the sugar and water in a small heavy-based saucepan and heat slowly until completely dissolved and clear, stirring once or twice. Meanwhile, whisk the egg yolks in a heatproof bowl using a hand-held electric mixer on full speed until pale yellow, thick and creamy. Increase the heat under the pan of sugar syrup and boil until it registers 120°C on a sugar thermometer; ie the 'hard ball stage', when a little of the hot syrup dropped into a glass of cold water forms a firm, clear ball. This should take 5–7 minutes. As soon as the syrup reaches this stage, remove from the heat.

2 With the electric beaters still whirring, trickle the just-boiled syrup on to the whisked egg yolks. Carry on whisking with the mixer on full speed so the mixture increases in volume and becomes thick, foamy and creamy. Place the bowl over a pan of simmering water and whisk for a further 5 minutes until the mixture is thick and glossy, and stands in floppy round peaks. Remove the bowl from the heat and continue whisking until the mixture has cooled to room temperature; it should be softly stiff. Allow to cool.

3 To make the Italian meringue, put the sugar, glucose and water in a small heavy-based saucepan and dissolve over a gentle heat. Meanwhile, whisk the egg whites in a clean bowl to the soft peak stage. Continue to boil the syrup until it reaches a temperature of 120°C, or the 'hard ball stage' (see above). With the beaters working on slow speed, trickle the boiling syrup on to the beaten egg whites. Continue whisking for about 5 minutes longer until cooled to room temperature.

4 Whiz the chopped mango and apricots to a purée in a blender or food processor. Pass through a sieve into a bowl, rubbing the purée through with the back of a ladle. Stir in the mint.

5 Melt the chocolate in a heatproof bowl over a pan of simmering water and stir until smooth. Cool to room temperature, stirring occasionally.

6 Fold the fruit purée into the pâte à bombe. Lightly fold the cooled chocolate into the meringue, then carefully fold in the creamy fruit mixture.

7 Finally, whip the cream until softly stiff and fold into the mousse. Spoon into glasses and chill to set. I like to serve these decadent mousses topped with caramelised mango slices.

Pumpkin cheesecake

This is a lightly baked cheesecake, cooked on a thin disc of sponge. It is best served simply with a light dusting of icing sugar, though you could add an indulgent spoonful of mascarpone. For a rich pumpkin flavour, prepare the purée ahead and freeze it. On thawing, the pulp separates out and you can discard the watery fluid leaving full-flavoured pumpkin flesh. **SERVES 6–8**

Sponge base
3 medium free-range eggs, separated
70g caster sugar
40g cornflour
40g strong plain flour

Filling
about 700g fresh unpeeled pumpkin
50g butter
100g caster or light soft brown sugar

200g mascarpone
125ml crème fraîche
70ml soured cream
seeds from 2 vanilla pods, or 1 teaspoon
  vanilla extract
2 large free-range eggs, separated

To serve
icing sugar, sifted, for dusting

1 First, prepare the pumpkin purée for the filling. Remove the seeds and stringy centre from the pumpkin, then peel away the skin as thinly as possible. Cut the flesh into small cubes. Heat the butter in a frying pan, add the pumpkin with 25g of the sugar and cook for about 10 minutes until softened. Transfer to a food processor and work until smooth. Allow to cool. You can make this purée a day or so ahead and freeze it to concentrate the flavour (see above).

2 For the sponge base, preheat the oven to 200°C, Gas 6. Whisk the egg whites in a bowl until softly stiff. Gradually fold in the caster sugar, then the egg yolks. Sift the cornflour and flour together over the mixture and then fold in carefully.

3 Line a baking sheet with baking parchment. Spread the sponge mixture out to an area approximately 30cm square – it needs to be an even thickness, but not necessarily a neat square. Bake for 7–10 minutes until golden brown and springy when pressed. Invert on to a wire rack to cool and then peel off the paper. Lower the oven setting to 170°C, Gas 3.

4 For the cheesecake you will need a 23–24cm springform cake tin, that is about 6cm deep. Cut out a round from the sponge base to fit exactly inside the tin, using the base of the tin as a guide. It is preferable to cut the sponge a little larger and trim it to fit, rather than cut it smaller and leave gaps that the pumpkin filling might leak through.

5 For the filling, beat the mascarpone, crème fraîche, soured cream, 50g of the remaining sugar, the vanilla seeds (or extract) and 2 egg yolks together in a bowl until evenly blended. Stir in the pumpkin purée.

6 Whisk the 2 egg whites in another bowl until softly stiff. Gradually whisk in the remaining 25g sugar and gently fold into the pumpkin mixture. Pour the filling over the sponge base in the tin and bake for 40–50 minutes until lightly firm on top.

7 Leave the cheesecake to cool and then chill in the tin. When ready to serve, run a table knife around the inside of the tin and carefully unmould on to a flat plate. Serve cut into wedges, dusted lightly with icing sugar.

Chocolate mocha tart

There are three parts to this tart: a smooth chocolate-topped pastry base, a light coffee and liqueur soaked sponge, and a rich velvety chocolate custard. Make the tart case and sponge disc ahead, leaving the topping until a few hours before serving. **SERVES 6–8**

1 quantity Sweet flan pastry (page 185)
200g dark chocolate (about 60% cocoa solids),
  melted

Sponge layer
1 large free-range egg white
2 teaspoons powdered egg white
40g caster sugar
50g ground almonds
1 tablespoon plain flour, sifted
2 tablespoons coffee essence
2 tablespoons Tia Maria

Mocha custard
120ml double cream
4 tablespoons milk
2 tablespoons strong fresh coffee, cooled
1 large free-range egg, beaten
50g caster sugar

1 To make a template for the sponge layer, line a baking sheet with baking parchment. Lay the removable base of a 21cm flan tin on top and draw round it. Return the base to the flan tin.
2 Roll out the pastry on a lightly floured surface and use to line the 21cm flan tin, which must be 3–3.5cm deep. As the dough is soft you may find it easier to pat it out after some initial rolling; pinch any cracks together. Don't trim the edge, leave it overhanging. Prick the base, then line with foil and baking beans. Chill for 15–20 minutes. Preheat oven to 190°C, Gas 5.
3 Put the flan tin on a baking sheet and bake blind for 15 minutes. Remove foil and beans, trim the pastry edge level with the top of the tin and bake for a further 10 minutes until crisp. Cool.
4 Turn the oven setting down to 170°C, Gas 3. Spread a third of the melted chocolate evenly over the pastry base. Keep the remaining chocolate runny, at room temperature.
5 Now make the sponge layer. Whisk the egg white and powdered egg white in a bowl until softly stiff, then whisk in the sugar until glossy and firm. Using a large metal spoon, carefully fold in the ground almonds and flour. Spread (or pipe) the mixture over the circle on the parchment. Bake for 12 minutes. Leave to stand for 5 minutes, then carefully peel off the paper and cool on a wire rack. Heat the coffee essence and liqueur until hot (not boiling), then cool.
6 For the custard, bring the cream and milk to the boil in a pan, then pour on to the remaining melted chocolate, stirring until smooth. Cool, then stir in the coffee. Beat the egg with the sugar, then mix with the chocolate cream.
7 When ready to assemble, heat the oven to 150°C, Gas 2. Fit the sponge disc into the pastry case and spoon over the coffee liqueur syrup. Put the flan tin on its baking sheet on the middle oven shelf, pulling the shelf out as far as it is safe. Pour in the chocolate custard – to reach the top. Gently push the oven shelf back and bake for about 40 minutes. The filling will be soft; on cooling it becomes firmer. Cool until the filling is the consistency of softly whipped cream.
8 Carefully unmould the tart on to a large flat plate and serve at room temperature.

Orange and lemon tart

I blush to say I am frequently complimented on the orange and lemon tart we serve at my restaurant – I must share the credit with my pâtisserie chefs, led by Thierry Besselieur. The perfect French lemon tart really depends on the skill of the cook, rolling out the rich sweet pastry until very thin without it breaking, boiling the fruit juices to concentrate the flavour and then baking the filling at a very low temperature until it is just softly set. As a final flourish, we add the thinnest crisp sugar crust, made not just with one caramelised sugar dusting, but two. Try it. SERVES 4–6

1 quantity Sweet flan pastry (page 185)
2 tablespoons icing sugar
Confit of Orange and Lemon (page 186), optional

Filling
600ml orange juice
juice of 2 lemons
grated zest of 1 lemon
grated zest of 1 orange
180g caster sugar
6 free-range egg yolks, beaten
150ml double cream

1 Roll out the pastry dough as thinly as you are able, to a round about 30cm in diameter, large enough to line a 20cm flan tin, 2.5–3cm deep, comfortably with overhang. You could do this on a lightly floured board, or between two lightly floured sheets of cling film. Lift the dough on the rolling pin into the flan tin (or a flan ring set on a heavy, flat baking sheet). Press the dough well on to the bottom and sides of the tin and pinch together or patch any gaps with dough trimmings. There should be a fair amount of overhang (don't trim it off). Place the tin on a baking sheet.

2 Fit a large sheet of foil into the pastry case, bringing it well up the sides. Fill with baking beans. Chill for 20 minutes, whilst you preheat the oven to 180°C, Gas 4.

3 Bake the pastry case blind for 12–15 minutes until just set. Remove the foil and beans. Return the pastry case to the oven to bake for 5 more minutes. Trim the top of the pastry case level with the tin using a very sharp knife, then set aside to cool whilst you make the filling.

4 Reduce the oven temperature to its lowest setting, ideally 100°C. (Many domestic ovens don't get this low and hover around 120°C.) Allow about 20 minutes for the temperature to fall.

5 For the filling, boil the orange and lemon juices together until reduced to about 170ml. Cool. Beat the lemon and orange zest with the sugar and egg yolks. Add the cream and then the cooled juice.

6 Place the pastry case on the pulled-out oven shelf and slowly pour in the filling, taking it up to as near the rim of the case as possible. Very, very carefully push the tart back into the oven and bake for about 35 minutes. The filling should still be quite soft. Turn off the oven and leave

the tart to cool inside until it sets enough so that it can be removed without spilling. Cool completely until lightly set, then chill.

7 Sift half of the icing sugar over the top of the tart in an even layer. Immediately caramelise the sugar with a blow torch. Let this cool and crisp, then sift another layer of icing sugar on top and caramelise that. Leave to cool completely.

8 Carefully cut the tart into neat portions using a long, sharp knife, and serve with a trickle of pouring cream if you wish. We also like to add a decoration of confit of orange and lemon slices – the perfect complement.

Tiramisu

In the restaurant we sometimes pipe a tiramisu-style cream into little chocolate cases and serve them as petits fours. To make a traditional tiramisu, you layer the cream with sponge fingers dipped in a coffee rum sauce . Make sure you buy the proper Italian savoyardi biscuits as they hold their shape better when dipped and layered. **SERVES 6**

Vanilla cream
100g caster sugar
5 tablespoons water
3 free-range egg yolks
250g mascarpone
100ml crème fraîche
5 tablespoons Greek yogurt
1 vanilla pod
300ml double cream

To assemble
200ml strong fresh coffee, cooled
3 tablespoons rum
about 12 Italian sponge finger biscuits
50g dark chocolate, grated

1 To make the vanilla cream, put the sugar and water in a small heavy-based pan and dissolve over a low heat. Increase the heat and boil for about 5 minutes until the syrup reaches 120°C – the 'hard ball' stage, when a small teaspoonful of syrup dropped into ice-cold water forms a firm, clear ball.

2 Using a hand-held electric mixer, whisk the egg yolks in a heatproof bowl placed on a damp cloth to hold it steady. When the yolks start to become thick and pale, reheat the sugar syrup briefly and trickle it down the side of the bowl as you whisk. Continue to whisk for a further 3–4 minutes, then remove and cool.

3 Put the mascarpone, crème fraîche and Greek yogurt in a bowl. Slit the vanilla pod open and scrape out the seeds, adding them to the bowl. Beat well, then gently mix into the cooled egg yolk mixture.

4 Whip the cream in a bowl until softly stiff, then fold into the mixture with a large metal spoon. Cover and chill until ready to serve.

5 To assemble, mix the coffee and rum together in a shallow bowl. Quickly dunk half of the sponge fingers in the liquid, one at a time, and make a single layer in a glass bowl. Spoon over half the tiramisu cream. Dunk the remaining sponge fingers in the same way and arrange on top. Spoon over the remaining cream, then dredge with the grated chocolate.

6 Chill for at least 2 hours before serving. Wait for the accolades.

Peach and cherry trifles

A good trifle should have the texture of a fruit fool – creamy without being at all runny. My favourite trifle has a base of macaroons (or amaretti biscuits) soaked in framboise, layers of sliced fresh peaches and red fruits, and a rich crème anglaise topping that has been whipped to lighten it. For a decadent finish, you can pile floppy whipped cream on top. (Note that this crème anglaise is richer than my standard recipe on page 185.) **SERVES 6**

Crème anglaise
300ml double cream
100ml milk
50g caster sugar
1 vanilla pod
6 large free-range egg yolks

Trifle
2 large ripe peaches
100g macaroons or amaretti biscuits

6 tablespoons framboise eau-de-vie,
   or medium dry sherry
150g pitted cherries, raspberries or
   other red fruit

To serve (optional)
150ml whipping cream
2 teaspoons icing sugar

1 First, prepare the crème anglaise. Put the cream and milk into a heavy-based pan with 1 tablespoon of the sugar. Slit the vanilla pod open and scrape out the seeds with the tip of a knife, adding them to the pan. Slowly bring to the boil. Meanwhile, beat the remaining sugar and egg yolks together in a large bowl, then gradually pour on a third of the creamy milk, beating constantly. Gradually pour in the rest of the milk mixture, whisking continuously.

2 Return this mixture to the pan and cook on a low heat, stirring continuously with a wooden spoon until the custard is thick enough to thinly coat the back of the spoon. Strain the custard into a clean bowl, cover and cool, then chill.

3 Skin the peaches for the trifle: dip in boiling water for 30 seconds then into cold water; remove and slip off the skins. Halve and stone the peaches, then slice thinly.

4 Crush the macaroons or amaretti biscuits and divide between 6 wine glasses. Sprinkle over the framboise or sherry and press the biscuits down lightly. Layer the sliced peaches and red fruit on top. Chill for 30 minutes.

5 Using a balloon whisk or electric whisk, beat the chilled crème anglaise until fluffy, then divide between the wine glasses.

6 To finish, whip the cream with the icing sugar, if using, and spoon on top of each trifle. Serve lightly chilled.

Vacherins of strawberries with a passion fruit cream

A vacherin is a shallow basket of meringue filled with a flavoured whipped cream and fresh fruits such as wild strawberries or other berries. We like to bake these in a very low oven so the meringue merely dries out and remains brilliant white. Our ovens have pilot lights that maintain a really low heat, but modern domestic ovens aren't so lucky. If you happen to have a four-oven Aga, the lowest warming oven should do the honours. Otherwise turn your oven to a 'keep warm' setting and prop the door open slightly with a wooden spoon. If your vacherins bake pale cream before they crisp, don't despair – they will still taste fabulous. **SERVES 6**

3 large free-range egg whites
 (ideally about 1 week old)
small squeeze of lemon juice
150g caster sugar

Passion fruit cream
6 passion fruit
200g mascarpone
150ml crème fraîche

70ml soured cream
a little icing sugar, to sweeten (optional)
150ml double cream

To serve
about 250g mixed raspberries, redcurrants and
 sliced wild strawberries (or other small ones)
icing sugar, for dusting

1 Turn the oven to its lowest setting, 110°C, Gas ¼ maximum. Line two baking sheets with baking parchment or a silicone cooking liner. Draw 6 circles, 8cm in diameter, on the paper.
2 Whisk the egg whites with the lemon juice in a large clean bowl until they form firm peaks; do not over-whisk or they will become dry and grainy. Gradually whisk in the sugar, a tablespoonful at a time, to make a smooth, glossy meringue.
3 Spoon the meringue into a piping bag fitted with a 1–1.5cm plain nozzle. Pipe in concentric rounds to fill each drawn circle. Pipe 2 rings on the edge of each meringue disc to form baskets.
4 Bake for at least 2 hours, or up to 8 hours if you are using the heat of a pilot light. The exact time will depend on the temperature, but it is easy to tell when the baskets are cooked. Lift one with a palette knife: if it comes away cleanly, feels crisp on the outside and slightly soft inside, the baskets are ready. Leave on the baking sheet for 10 minutes, then carefully peel the meringue baskets off the paper and transfer to a wire rack to cool completely.
5 Meanwhile, make the passion fruit cream. Halve the passion fruit, scoop out the pulp and seeds into a small pan and boil to reduce by half and concentrate the flavour. Tip into a sieve over a bowl and rub with a wooden spoon to extract as much juice as possible; discard seeds.
6 Beat the mascarpone with the crème fraîche and soured cream. Mix in the passion fruit juice and sweeten with a little icing sugar, if required. Whip the double cream until it is softly stiff and then fold into the passion fruit cream.
7 When ready to serve, spoon the passion fruit cream into the meringue baskets and top with the fruits. A light dusting of icing sugar adds a magical touch.

Basic recipes

Light chicken stock

Place 3kg raw chicken carcasses or bony joints in a large stockpot. Add a good 5 litres of cold water, 3 quartered onions, 2 chopped leeks, 2 large chopped carrots, 4 chopped celery sticks, 1 small head garlic (cut in half widthways), 1 large sprig fresh thyme and 1 tablespoon sea salt. Bring slowly to the boil, skimming off any scum that rises using a large metal spoon (not slotted because the scum can drain through). Boil for 5 minutes, then turn the heat right down and simmer for 3–4 hours. Cool and allow the solids to settle. Line a colander with a sheet of wet muslin and place over a bowl. Slowly pour the stock through. Cool, then chill. This stock can be kept in the fridge for up to 3 days or frozen. Makes about 3 litres.

For **dark chicken stock**, first roast the chicken carcasses in a preheated 200°C, Gas 6 oven for about 20 minutes, turning frequently. Drain off the fat and proceed as above.

Vegetable nage

One of the most useful stocks to have on hand, this is made slightly differently from other stocks.

Put the following ingredients into a large stockpot: 3 chopped onions, 6 chopped carrots, 2 chopped celery sticks, 1 chopped leek, 1 small head garlic (split in two widthways), 1 quartered lemon, $\frac{1}{4}$ teaspoon each white and pink peppercorns, 1 small bay leaf and 4 star anise. Pour in 2 litres of cold water, bring slowly to the boil and simmer for 10 minutes.

Remove from the heat and mix in 200ml dry white wine. Add a sprig each of fresh tarragon, basil, coriander, thyme and curly-leaf parsley. Cool, then decant into a large bowl and refrigerate for a good 24 hours. Strain through a muslin-lined colander. This can be kept in the fridge for up to 4 days or frozen. Makes about 1.5 litres.

Fish stock

White fish bones are the most useful, e.g. those from turbot, sole, haddock, hake and so on, not oily fish such as salmon. You'll need about 1.5–2kg of bones. If using fish heads too, cut out the eyes and the gills.

Gently sweat 1 small chopped onion, 1 chopped leek, 1 chopped celery stick, 1 small chopped bulb fennel and 2 whole garlic cloves in a little olive oil for 10 minutes. Add the fish bones (and heads) and 300ml dry white wine, and cook until the wine evaporates. Cover with about 3 litres of cold water, and add a fresh bouquet garni (bay leaf, sprig fresh thyme and some parsley stalks tied together), 1 small sliced lemon and a few white peppercorns. Bring to the boil, skimming well, then simmer for 20 minutes only – no longer or the stock will become bitter. Cool so the solids settle, then strain through a muslin-lined colander. This can be kept for up to 3 days in the fridge or frozen. Makes 2.5 litres.

Court bouillon

Use this for poaching lobsters and whole fish. It can be used up to three times, straining in between.

Simply put all of the following ingredients into a large stockpot: 2 chopped leeks, 3 chopped carrots, 3 chopped onions, 2 chopped celery sticks, 2 chopped bulbs fennel and 4 large garlic cloves (unpeeled). Cover with about 3 litres of cold water and add 1 large sprig each fresh thyme, parsley, basil and tarragon, plus 1 tablespoon sea salt, 2 sliced lemons, 4 star anise and 300ml dry white wine. Bring to the boil, then simmer gently for 30 minutes. Strain through a muslin-lined colander. This can be kept for up to 5 days in the fridge or frozen. Makes about 1.5 litres.

Vinaigrette

This has many uses apart from dressing salads.

Whisk together 200ml extra virgin olive oil and 200ml groundnut oil with 1 teaspoon fine sea salt, $\frac{1}{4}$ teaspoon ground black pepper, the juice of 1 lemon, 50ml white wine vinegar and 50ml sherry vinegar. Store the vinaigrette in a large screw-topped jar and shake to re-emulsify before use. Makes about 500ml.

Mayonnaise

Whisk 2 free-range egg yolks, 1 teaspoon white wine vinegar, 1 teaspoon English mustard powder and a little seasoning together in a bowl. (Sit the bowl on a damp cloth to hold it steady.) Using 300ml groundnut oil or half groundnut and half light olive oil, drop in a trickle from a teaspoon and beat hard until mixed. Continue like this, gradually adding a tad more oil each time, making sure the previous amount is well mixed in before adding more. Gradually increase the amount of oil added as the mixture gets thicker and more creamy. When all of the oil is mixed in, whisk in 2 tablespoons cold water. Check the seasoning. The mayonnaise can be kept in a sealed container in the fridge for up to a week. Makes 300ml.

Stock syrup

I flavour stock syrups in various ways – you may find a strip or two of lemon zest is best for general uses, but other ingredients could include a split vanilla pod, a cinnamon stick, or even a split stalk of lemon grass.

Slowly dissolve 250g caster sugar in 500ml water. When the sugar syrup is clear, add the flavouring and simmer for 5 minutes; cool. This stock syrup will keep for a month in the fridge. Makes 700ml.

Sweet flan pastry

This is one of the standard pastries we use for sweet tarts. I always roll out more pastry than is needed to line the tin, to allow for shrinkage.

Using an electric mixer, beat 100g unsalted butter with 70g caster sugar until smooth and creamy. Scrape out the seeds from a split vanilla pod and add them to the creamed mixture. Work in 1 beaten medium egg and 200g plain flour sifted with a pinch of salt, alternately until you have a smooth dough. Gather the dough and knead gently on a lightly floured surface for a minute or two, then wrap in cling film and rest in the fridge for 20 minutes. Makes 400g.

Puff pastry

Bought puff pastry may be convenient and good at rising evenly, but nothing beats home-made for buttery flavour and melt-in-the-mouth texture. Make this in a large batch and freeze in easy-to-use blocks.

Divide 500g chilled butter into 450g and 50g. Do the same with 500g of plain flour sifted with ¼ teaspoon salt. Cut the 450g of butter into small dice and mix with the 50g flour (ideally in a food processor). Spoon onto a large sheet of cling film and shape into a large rectangle about 14 x 20cm; try to keep the edges neat. Set aside.

Rub the 50g butter into the 450g of flour. (This is best done in a food processor.) Trickle in 1 teaspoon of fresh lemon juice and enough ice-cold water so the mixture just comes together in a mass – this may take up to 300ml of water, added gradually. Knead lightly to a smooth dough. Roll out on a lightly floured board to a rectangle about 25 x 35cm, keeping the edges neat and straight with even corners. Place the butter rectangle on one side and fold over the other half of the dough to enclose it. Press the edges to seal.

Carefully roll out the dough until it is about three times as long as it is wide. Make sure the butter doesn't break through. Now, fold the top third down and fold the bottom third over it, like a blanket. Give the dough a quarter turn and roll out again, dusting lightly with flour as necessary. Fold again into three, and wrap in cling film. Chill to rest for 20 minutes, then repeat the rolling and folding twice more. Try to remember to do the folding and turning

in the same direction. Divide the pastry dough into two or three portions as required and wrap in cling film. Freeze portions that you are not using now. Makes 1.2kg.

Crème anglaise

If you have never made a rich custard before, you might want to have a large bowl of iced water at the ready, so you can plunge the base of the pan into it to cool it quickly. Another useful hint is that you can use a sugar thermometer or instant-read thermometer to check if the custard is cooked enough – the temperature should be 82°C.

Slit a vanilla pod in half and scoop out the seeds on the lip of the knife. Put 250ml each milk and double cream in a heavy-based saucepan and mix in the vanilla seeds. Add the pod too. Heat until the liquid starts to rise up in the pan, then remove from the heat and allow to infuse for 10 minutes.

Meanwhile, put 6 free-range egg yolks and 90g caster sugar in a large bowl set on a damp cloth (to hold it steady) and beat with a balloon whisk until pale golden and creamy. Remove the vanilla pod from the infused milk, then bring back to the boil. Tip the creamy milk in small slurps on to the sugar and yolks, whisking hard.

Return the mixture to the pan over the lowest heat possible. Stir with a wooden spoon for about 2 minutes until the custard starts to thicken – just enough to coat the back of the spoon. Don't overheat or it will curdle. Strain, cover with a disc of damp greaseproof paper and leave to cool, stirring occasionally to prevent a skin forming. Makes 600ml.

Confit of orange and lemon

Heat 200ml Stock Syrup (page 185) to boiling. Meanwhile, slice 1 large seedless orange and 1 lemon evenly into 3mm discs, with the peel. Drop the fruit slices into the boiling syrup, then remove from the heat and allow to cool. Remove the confit slices as required; they can be kept in the fridge for up to a month in a covered container. When all the confit slices are gone, you can re-boil the syrup (it will be orange- and lemon-scented) and use again.

Confit of lemon and lime zest

Wash 3 lemons or 3 limes (or a combination of these), and pat dry. Finely pare the zest using a swivel vegetable peeler. Scrape off any pith, then cut the zest into thin julienne strips. Blanch the citrus zest in boiling water for 2 minutes, then drain and pat dry. Bring 250ml Stock syrup (page 185) to the boil in a small pan. Drop the citrus zest into the pan, bring back to the boil and simmer for 3 minutes. Remove from the heat and leave to cool. Spoon the zest strips and syrup into a screw-topped jar and store in the fridge for up to 1 month. Remove the zest to use when required.

Caramelised mango slices

These are superb with creamy ices and mousses. Peel and slice a mango, discarding the stone. Place in a shallow dish. Sift 1½ tablespoons icing sugar with a good pinch of Chinese five-spice powder spice together over the mangoes and toss the fruit to coat.

Gently heat a knob of butter with 2 teaspoons caster sugar in a heavy-based frying pan, stirring, until melted. Increase the heat and cook until the buttery syrup is a light caramel colour. Add the mango slices in a single layer and cook for about 5 minutes, turning once, until lightly browned on both sides. Leave to cool slightly in the pan juices. Serve warm.

Oven-dried fruit slices

First, make up a quantity of Stock syrup (page 185). Turn the oven on to its lowest setting. Line 2 baking sheets with a silicone cooking liner (such as silpat or bake-o-glide). Prepare your chosen fruit, such as peaches, plums, apples, mangoes, pears or pineapple. Only pineapples and mangoes should be peeled. Use a sharp serrated fruit knife to cut the fruit into wafer-thin slices. Apples and pears are best cored neatly, although pears can be sliced whole lengthways up to the core. Dip apples, pears and other fruits that are prone to discoloration into a little sugar syrup mixed with a squeeze of lemon juice as soon as you slice them.

Dip the fruit slices quickly into the stock syrup, shake off excess and lay on the silicone cooking liners. Leave in the low oven for a good 2 hours. If the fruit appears to be starting to brown, lower the temperature by propping open the door with a wooden spoon handle.

The slices are ready when they feel firm and can be lifted off easily. Don't leave them in the oven for longer than is necessary; they crisp up on cooling. Store the dried fruit slices in airtight plastic containers. If properly dried, they will keep crisp for at least a week.

Praline

Preheat the oven to 180°C, Gas 4. Warm 120g flaked almonds in the oven for 10 minutes. Meanwhile, melt 160g caster sugar in a saucepan with a splash of water until clear, stirring once or twice. Add a squeeze of lemon juice, then raise the heat and cook to a light caramel colour. Stir in the almonds, then pour on to a flat baking tray lined with non-stick baking parchment. Leave until cool and set. Crush with a rolling pin into chunks, then grind to very fine crumbs in a food processor. Store in a screw-topped jar and use as required – praline is a delicious topping for an icecream sundae. Makes 280g.

Glossary of culinary terms

BAIN-MARIE A water bath in which a dish is held during cooking to moderate the temperature so the mixture does not overcook or curdle, and the sides do not become crusty. In the oven a roasting tin half filled with boiling water serves as a bain-marie. On top of the stove, the mixture is placed in a heatproof bowl containing a 5–7cm depth of gently simmering water.

BAKING BEANS Dried pulses, such as lentils or haricot beans, used to weight down pastry during baking blind to prevent air bubbles. Ceramic baking beans, made especially for this purpose, are also available.

BAKING BLIND To bake an unfilled pastry flan case until cooked and crisp. The pastry dough is pressed into a flan tin, or flan ring on a baking sheet, covered with foil or baking parchment and filled with baking beans to stop it from rising.

BASTE To spoon the pan juices or a syrup over foods such as roasted fruit during cooking to keep them moist and encourage them to caramelise.

BIND To mix liquid such as beaten egg or water into pastry or other dry mixture to bring it together.

BLANCH To dip uncooked food into boiling water, syrup or hot oil very briefly to seal the outside or semi-cook it. This may take less than a minute, a few minutes at the most. The food is then refreshed (see overleaf).

BRULEE Literally translated as 'burnt', this term describes a cream-based sweet, sprinkled with an even layer of demerara or caster sugar, then caramelised – either by waving a kitchen blow-torch over the surface or by placing under a very hot grill.

BRUNOISE Very finely diced fruits.

CARAMELISE To heat melted sugar or sugar syrup until it colours and forms a caramel. The term also applies to food cooked in a hot dry pan so the natural sugars brown, enhancing the flavour. Sometimes fruits are brushed with softened butter and tossed in sugar first, to help the process.

CONFIT Fruits cooked very slowly submerged in syrup then served 'on the side' as a type of sweet relish. We confit the zest of citrus fruit to serve alongside tarts. Submerged in the syrup, this citrus confit keeps for a good 2–3 months in the fridge.

COULIS A smooth fruit sauce made with a fruit purée and stock syrup.

CURDLE Inadvertently, certain sauces and creamed mixtures can be separated by overheating, or mixing with acidic foods. Curdling is due to the proteins in cream or eggs coagulating and forming small lumps. To avoid this happening, heat-sensitive mixtures should be heated carefully and not allowed to boil. Alternatively, they may be stabilised with a little starch, such as cornflour.

DECANT To pour one liquid from a bottle into another bottle or jug. This is done slowly so any sediment in the base of the bottle is left behind and can be discarded.

DEGLAZE To pour a little alcohol or other liquid into a hot pan and stir vigorously to soften any residue and mix with the pan juices so they may be used for a sauce. The liquid evaporates away a little to concentrate the flavour. For example, a shot of wine may be used to deglaze a pan in which fruit has been caramelised in butter and sugar.

DUST To lightly sprinkle with icing sugar, flour, cocoa powder or ground spice, shaking from a fine sieve.

FILO A wafer-thin pastry dough that has been pulled into thin sheets, rather than rolled – sold in packets or boxes. It is assembled in layers with melted butter or oil. Filo must be kept covered to prevent it drying out.

FLAMBE To ignite a mixture containing alcohol – usually in a sauté pan – to burn off the alcohol, concentrating and mellowing the flavour.

FOLDING IN To combine at least two mixtures gently together with a large metal spoon to retain the light texture. The spoon is turned gently in a figure-of-eight action so that it scoops up and gently incorporates mixture from the base of the bowl without knocking out air. Usually one of the mixtures is whipped egg whites or cream.

GLAZE To apply a coating to food before or after cooking for an attractive shiny finish. Fruit may be glazed with coulis or sugar syrup. Pastry and bread are often glazed with beaten egg.

INFUSE To immerse flavouring ingredients – such as herbs, citrus zest or vanilla pods – in hot syrup, milk or other liquid to impart a subtle flavour and aroma. The flavourings are usually added to the just-boiled liquid and left to stand for a while to infuse before being removed.

JULIENNE Very thinly sliced strips of citrus fruit zest or leafy herbs.

JUS The pure extracted juice of fruit without additional water or syrup. We extract pure strawberry jus from berries over a bain-marie for example, and make an apple jus by sieving puréed fresh (uncooked) apples.

KNEAD To work a dough by hand on a lightly floured board. Most pastries are given a light kneading to make them smooth before rolling out. Bread doughs are kneaded more vigorously to develop the gluten.

LET DOWN To thin a liquid or mixture with a thinner one.

MACERATE To steep fruits in a liquid, usually syrup or alcohol, to flavour and soften them.

MI-CUIT Dried fruits, such as prunes or apricots, that have been partially cooked so they do not necessarily require soaking before use.

PARBOIL To boil a vegetable or other item for part of its cooking time before finishing it by another method.

PARE To thinly peel the skin or zest from fruit, using a small, sharp knife or vegetable peeler, so that only the zest is removed, not the pith.

POACH To cook food in a liquid that is kept just below boiling point. The liquid should barely bubble. For example, fruit may be poached in a light stock syrup so that it remains whole.

PUREE To blend or sieve food, such as fruit, to a smooth pulp. Soft berry fruits and bananas can be puréed raw, other fruits may need to be cooked lightly to soften them first.

REDUCE To boil liquid, such as fruit juice, in an uncovered wide pan to evaporate some of the water and concentrate the flavour.

REFRESH To place food that has been just blanched into ice-cold water to stop any further cooking and bring down the temperature rapidly.

RIBBON STAGE Whisking egg yolks and sugar, often over a bain-marie, until the mixture forms a foam that is thick enough to leave a trail when some of the mixture is lifted up on the whisk and falls back into the bowl.

SCALDING POINT To bring milk and/or cream to just below boiling point. Scalding point is reached once the liquid starts to froth around the edge of the pan, just before it starts to creep up

the sides. At this stage take it off the heat immediately.

STEEP To soak ingredients in liquid, usually to soften them, or sometimes to draw out strong flavours.

STRAIN To pass a liquid through a sieve to make sure it is entirely free of tiny particles. Sometimes it is necessary to rub the liquid through the sieve using the back of a ladle.

SWEAT To cook sliced or chopped vegetables in a little fat without liquid in a covered pan over a low heat to soften them.

WHIPPING Incorporating air into an ingredient or mixture by beating rapidly with a balloon whisk or electric whisk. Ingredients such as cream and egg whites may be whipped to various stages – lightly thickened, softly stiff, or stiff peaks, for example. Three-quarters whipped cream that is whipped until thickened and forms light soft floppy peaks is the ideal texture for folding into mousses.

Index

ACKNOWLEDGEMENTS
Consultant Anne Furniss
Art Director Helen Lewis
Project Editors Janet Illsley and Norma Macmillan
Food Stylist Mark Sargeant
Pâtisserie Chef Thierry Besselieure
Design Assistant Ros Holder
Editorial Assistant Jane Keskeys
Production Beverley Richardson